WINDSOR REVEALED

New light on the history of the castle

Steven Brindle and Brian Kerr

ENGLISH HERITAGE

Contents

Published by English Heritage, 23 Savile Row, London W1X 1AB
© English Heritage 1997 First published 1997
Edited by Lorimer Poultney Designed by Pauline Hull
Printed in England by The White Dove Press
ISBN 1 85074 688 5
A catalogue record for this publication is available from the
British Library

Acknowledgements
Unless otherwise stated all photographs were taken by English
Heritage and remain the copyright of English Heritage. Illustrations
from the Royal Collection are reproduced by gracious permission
of Her Majesty the Queen. Drawings provided by Dave Fellows,
Steven Brindle and John Pidgeon were enhanced for publication
by Vince Griffin and John Vallender.
  The authors are grateful for contributions from Jennifer Hillam,
Paul Bryan, Sarah Lunnon, Sophie Stewart and John Pidgeon,
and advice from John Thorneycroft, Geoff Wainwright, Dave
Batchelor, Adrian Olivier, Glynis Edwards, Sarah Jennings and Jan
Summerfield. Particular thanks go to all those who worked on the
Round Tower and fire restoration projects.

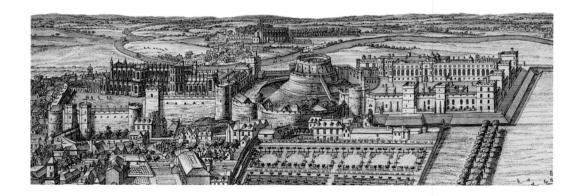

*ABOVE Windsor Castle from the south; engraving
from* Britannia Illustrata, *1711
RIGHT Windsor Castle from the air (Aerofilms)*

WINDSOR REVEALED

Foreword

The fire at Windsor Castle on 20 November 1992 shocked the nation. Few will forget that famous skyline ablaze, the terrible scene of devastation afterwards, and Her Majesty the Queen's visit to her stricken castle. Fortunately, our great national symbols as are resilient as our nation. Windsor is not our oldest royal residence for nothing. Five years to the day after the disaster, the greatest historic building restoration project in Britain this century was declared complete, on time and under budget. It is a triumph of British craftsmanship, and a credit to the Royal Household and to everyone who has worked on it.

English Heritage is proud to have been associated with the restoration from the onset. On the day after the fire, English Heritage staff were on site to help the Royal Household assess the damage and to begin the emergency work. Since then, almost the whole range of our professional expertise – architectural and historical advisers, archaeologists, surveyors, painting conservators and others – has been drawn on by the Royal Household and their Project Team.

By chance, three weeks before the fire our archaeologists had just completed a three-year investigation of Windsor's Round Tower. Now they returned to the Castle for a greater task. Their work has transformed our view of the Castle and its history. Windsor used to be seen largely as a creation of the Gothic Revival. The fire, which burnt off layers of nineteenth-century plaster and panelling, has revealed the true complexity of the building beneath, and its more than eight hundred years of history.

So much evidence has been amassed that analysing and publishing it to academic standards will take some while. In the meantime, this book sets out to convey our main discoveries, while explaining something of the techniques and methods used, to as wide a readership as possible. Samuel Pepys described Windsor as 'the most Romantique castle that is in the world'. Our new understanding of the Castle enhances its romance.

Sir Jocelyn Stevens, CVO
Chairman, English Heritage

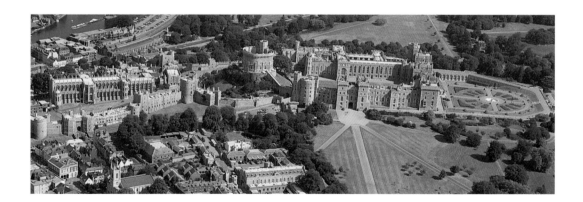

INTRODUCTION

The archaeological context

Paul Sandby's watercolour painting of the Round Tower, c.1790, before Wyatville increased its height

Windsor is one of Britain's greatest castles, with a history of building, occupation and development spread over 900 years. Since 1913, our understanding of the castle's history has relied on the work of Sir William St John Hope, who combined an architectural study of the castle with an analysis of the documentary history to produce a model for the castle's development. Archaeological investigation of Windsor Castle before the end of the 1980s had been limited: there was an excavation of the site of the Great Hall in the Lower Ward in 1895, and excavations at the side of the motte and at the western end of St George's Chapel during the 1970s. Between 1989 and 1997, and especially in the period after the fire in November 1992, intensive archaeological investigation of parts of the castle has started to revolutionise previously held views. This summary will reveal some of the recent discoveries that are contributing to a new understanding of this great royal palace.

1989–92: the Round Tower

Windsor Castle is divided into two main parts, the Upper and Lower Wards, by the huge chalk mound or 'motte': the only part of William the Conqueror's earthwork fortification still visible today. The timber defences of this early castle were thought to have been replaced by the stone shell keep – a curtain-wall of masonry built around the edge of the summit – by the late twelfth century, and continued to be occupied in this form until the tower was heightened by the architect Jeffry Wyatville in the early nineteenth century.

The huge weight of the heightened tower and its contents eventually proved too much for the motte, which is simply a large pile of chalk rubble, and in the winter of 1987–88 the foundations of the tower began to move. The problem was a serious one – if left alone, the continuing movement would have led to the tower's collapse. The solution was a drastic one. The foundations were to be replaced by a new concrete ring-beam foundation, standing on a series of piles drilled through the motte into the chalk bedrock below. This work was clearly going to be enormously destructive to the archaeology of the tower, and so a programme of excavation and recording was included in the underpinning project.

The results of the investigations surpassed expectations. A superb sequence of buildings from the late eleventh to the mid-fourteenth centuries was excavated, and this was linked with the discovery that the present Round Tower is the second large stone building of its type on the top of the motte. The recording of the buildings within the tower confirmed that the fourteenth-century timber-framed ranges survived, and much new information on their layout and design was revealed.

The long archaeological project in the Round Tower drew to an end at the beginning of November 1992. Little did we know at the topping-out ceremony that we would soon be back at the castle, this time in the aftermath of the disastrous fire which destroyed a large part of the Upper Ward less than three weeks later.

The Round Tower after Wyatville's rebuilding. A photograph of c.1850 attributed to William Henry Fox-Talbot

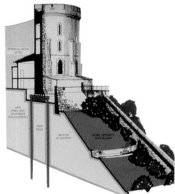

ABOVE Diagram showing how the tower was to be underpinned

TOP LEFT Survey work within the roof space

BELOW LEFT Excavation in the central courtyard of the Round Tower

WINDSOR DEVASTATED

The day after the fire

The fire that broke out on the night of 20 November 1992 destroyed a large area at the heart of the historic palace. Starting in the private Royal Chapel, at the centre of a complex set of buildings with interconnecting roof spaces, the fire spread all the way from St George's Hall in the west to the Chester Tower in the south, destroying the entire north-eastern corner of the palace. The effects of this calamity varied across the site. Close to the seat of the fire, the buildings were very heavily damaged, with the roofs destroyed and the wall-linings burnt off to reveal the masonry and brickwork behind them. Elsewhere, the fire flashed through the roof spaces, destroying ceilings but leaving the walls largely intact. In most places, the fire was confined to first-floor level and above, the ground floor being protected by a mixture of medieval stone vaulting and iron, brick and stone floors from the nineteenth century. However, single-storey buildings in the Kitchen Court area were also gutted, including the huge Royal Kitchen itself.

The immediate concern was the effect of the fire on the buildings. Another and more insidious effect, however, was the saturation of the historic buildings with water, as a result of the fire-fighting operation and exposure to the winter weather before the temporary roof was in place. These conditions provided an ideal opportunity for the spread of rot, and it was clear that the palace could not be restored until the walls had dried out. This led to the stripping of render and plasterwork from large areas of the ground floor, and the removal of panelling from relatively undamaged sections of the upper floors, leading to a much greater exposure of the underlying fabric of the palace.

The fire was a disaster, and much of the important interior design of the early nineteenth century was destroyed. As work progressed, it became clear that earlier remains had also been badly damaged. It was soon apparent, however, that important medieval features had been exposed, providing an unparalled opportunity to learn much more about the castle's history.

Archaeologists from English Heritage were back on site the day after the fire. Not only had we learned a lot about the development of the castle buildings from our work at the Round Tower, but we had also helped to tackle the aftermath of major fires in historic buildings, at Hampton Court Palace in 1986 and at Uppark, West Sussex, in 1989. With the agreement of the Government and of the Royal Household, the techniques developed in the clearance of these buildings were employed at Windsor, in order to provide information that would eventually assist in the reconstruction of the buildings.

REX FEATURES

ABOVE Firefighters tackling the fire in its early stages

RIGHT Outline plan of the castle, showing the extent of the fire-damaged area

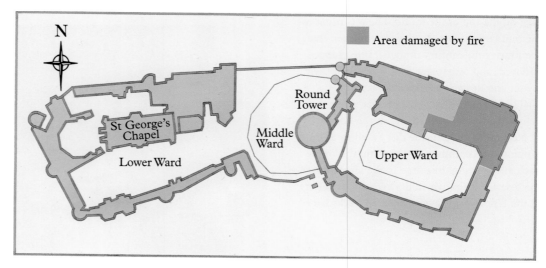

N

Area damaged by fire

St George's Chapel

Lower Ward

Middle Ward

Round Tower

Upper Ward

*FAR LEFT Looking down
on the fire-damaged area*

*LEFT The burnt-out
St George's Hall*

*BELOW The Grand
Reception Room*

THE SALVAGE OPERATION

Clearing the building

Work began immediately after the fire had been extinguished. Floors throughout the building were covered in a thick layer of soggy debris, comprised of plasterwork, glass, charcoal and charred wood from the damaged floor and roof structures, and lead from the roof coverings. All of this material had to be removed as soon as possible so that other work could start, but from previous experience we knew that this smelly and unpromising-looking debris contained a great deal of material which would help in the reconstruction of the buildings.

The aim of the salvage operation was to recover as much information as possible about the pre-fire structure and decoration. How the rooms were to be reconstructed was not immediately clear, and indeed was a matter of some public debate, but in these early stages it was important not to limit the options for reconstruction. If authentic restoration was to be the way forward, then the recovery of the information contained within the sodden and charred debris was essential. This included the major structures, such as roofs and floors, and in some places walls which had collapsed. There were also huge quantities of plaster from highly decorated rooms such as the Grand Reception Room, painted window glass, chandeliers, furniture, decorative fittings, and some sculptures. Fortunately the apartments above the main rooms had been empty, and we were not faced with the additional difficult work of recovering personal possessions from the debris.

The approach taken was to evaluate each of the major rooms in terms of its historic importance, the nature of its pre-fire decoration, and a list of the fittings and contents provided by the Royal Collection. For each area a salvage strategy was then drawn up, with varying levels of sift depending on what was to be recovered from each room. St George's Hall was identified as a low-level sift area; the room had been empty at the time of the fire, and the ceiling plaster had been of poor quality and had not survived. The debris was removed systematically,

ABOVE General view of salvage in St George's Hall

OPPOSITE Charred plaster coving ornament with royal coat-of-arms from the Grand Reception Room

with timbers and metalwork retained for further examination, but none of the fine debris was kept for further processing.

An example of the highest level of sift was the Grand Reception Room. All of the plaster from the ceilings was to be recovered, and in addition there were three chandeliers in the debris, and fragments of malachite veneer from the Malachite Urn, presented to the Royal Family by Tsar Nicholas I in 1844. The value of collecting all of the pieces of glass from the chandeliers was not clear at the time of the

salvage work, but this material has since been re-used. Malachite from the urn was the highest priority, and we were instructed to recover every fragment for restoration. The room was gridded to record the approximate location of the plasterwork; the siting of the plasterwork within the debris depended as much on the way the ceiling collapsed as it did on its original location within the ceiling, and so it was not worth recording in great detail. The plasterwork was stored in plastic bread-trays, which were strong enough to hold the heavy plaster in stacks, and at the same time allowed air to circulate around the damp contents to start the drying-out process.

Further grid boxes were laid out around the Urn and the chandelier locations to allow for a more thorough search of this material. Where a fine search was required, the debris was taken off site in plastic dustbins where it was sorted in our processing area at the Mushroom Farm (see page 10). The benefit of this approach was that most of the material was sorted on site, with only the bare minimum of unsorted debris removed for processing off-site.

This method worked well where the archaeological team had access to the debris, but there were large sections of the castle which were declared too dangerous to be cleared in this way. In these rooms, including the Green and Crimson Drawing Rooms and the State Dining Room, the clearance of the debris was carried out by demolition contractors working to the archaeologists' specification, but the entire contents of these rooms were carted off-site in dustbins for sorting and detailed analysis at the Mushroom Farm, greatly increasing the work which had to be done there.

Objects being recovered from St George's Hall

Excavating the chandelier in the Grand Reception Room. Note how the candles had survived intact, since they were below the fire

The salvage process in the Private Chapel

Sorting the debris

The debris removed from the castle was taken to the Mushroom Farm, a group of agricultural buildings within the Home Park. These provided a large covered working area and suitable buildings for the storage of the material. When at its busiest, vans were shuttling to and from the castle on a regular basis, bringing full dustbins and bread-trays down for processing, and taking the 'empties' back to the castle.

For the dustbins full of debris, sorting was a relatively straightforward procedure. The contents of the bins were tipped one at a time onto a moving conveyor, and archaeologists picked the plaster, glass and other items out of the debris as it passed, with the residue going straight into a skip at the end. This system had been developed at Uppark, where the conveyor fed a mechanical sieve, but experience there had shown that such a high percentage of the material could be recovered from the belt by

hand that the mechanical sieve was not needed. Once collected, the finds were sorted into their constituent materials, and stored in the bread trays. The finds were recorded, with information on their material and location entered onto a computerised database, so that the material could be quickly located when it was needed.

The finds were still damp, and had to be dried out before fungal growths could take hold. The storeroom was initially dry, but within days of the first trays being moved in, the walls were dripping with water. The stores were fitted out with dehumidifiers, and these soon allowed the material to dry out without further damage. Some of the recovered material was taken away immediately by the Royal Household for conservation, including the remains of statuary and furniture, but much of the rest remained in store until it was needed for the reconstruction project some two to three years later.

RIGHT Collecting material in bread-trays ready for transportation to the Mushroom Farm

FAR RIGHT The moving conveyor used to sort debris

BELOW General view of the sorting area at the Mushroom Farm

Roofs and timberwork

The first work to be undertaken in the aftermath of the fire was making the site safe. Roof and floor structures had been burnt out throughout the damaged area, and many were in a very precarious state. It was clear that badly damaged structures had to be removed as soon as possible, and that we would have to record these as best we could, safety permitting. We therefore drew up our priorities for recording within the first few days, looking at the damaged structures to determine which were the most important and which were the most vulnerable.

Most of the roofs were of nineteenth-century or later date; this did not mean that they were unimportant, but it did mean that in many cases there were records of their construction, and these could be combined with a minimal level of recording to allow their accurate reconstruction if that were required. An example of this approach was the roof of the Chester Tower, dating from Wyatville's work

of the 1820s. The roof was photographed as it survived the fire and during demolition, but it was too unsafe to be recorded where it stood. The trusses were dismantled by demolition contractors, and laid out on the ground in the Quadrangle where they could be drawn in detail.

Charred trusses from St George's Hall, with their iron reinforcement bars

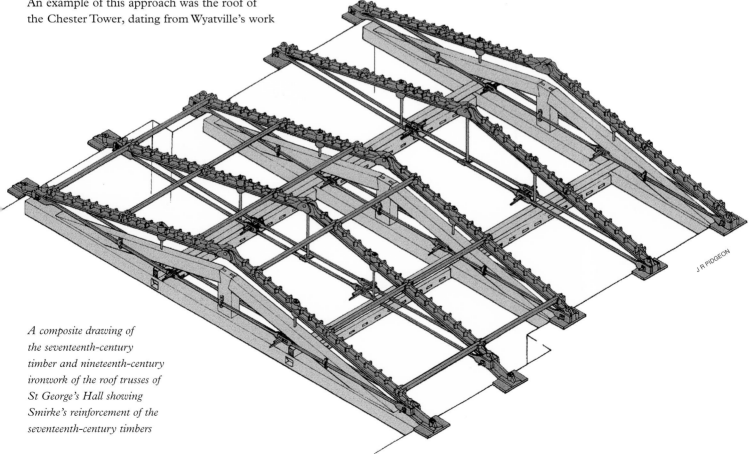

J R PIDGEON

A composite drawing of the seventeenth-century timber and nineteenth-century ironwork of the roof trusses of St George's Hall showing Smirke's reinforcement of the seventeenth-century timbers

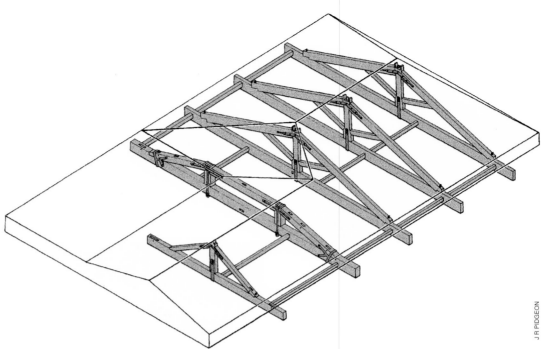

RIGHT *Post-fire drawing of Chester Tower roof frame*

BELOW *Wyatville's construction drawing of the roof frame of the Chester Tower*

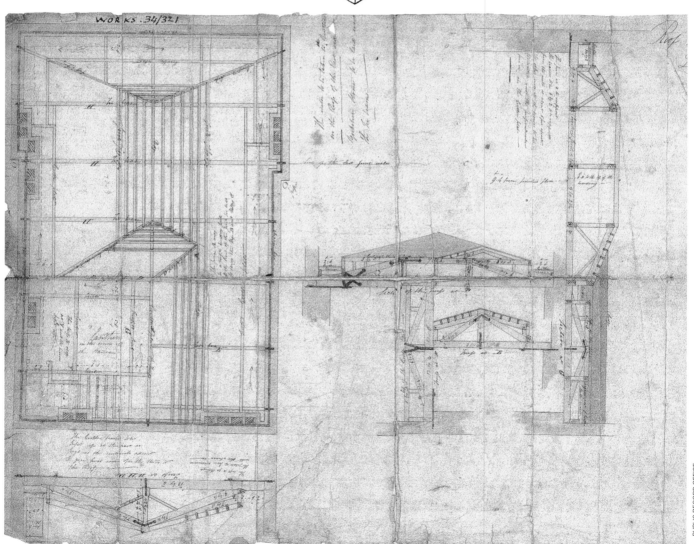

Combined with Wyatville's drawings, a full drawn reconstruction of the roof was immediately possible. This roof was ultimately replaced in steel, and thus our drawings form a final record of the destroyed roof.

An important discovery was that the timber roof of St George's Hall was of late seventeenth-century date, and that it had been reinforced with an elaborate cast- and wrought-iron superstructure in 1824 by Robert Smirke. Most of this had to be dismantled for safety reasons, and indeed several of the trusses had collapsed during the fire. These trusses were removed from site and stored at the Mushroom Farm, where they could be recorded safely and at leisure.

The roof of the Grand Reception Room was a nineteenth-century composite structure of softwood trusses with iron bracing. This had been charred, but had not collapsed, and for a long time it was thought that it could be saved. However, closer examination showed that many of the joints had been burnt-out, and that they could not support the weight of the restored roof-leads and plaster ceiling. This roof was recorded in place before it was dismantled.

Other roofs did not have to be recorded at all, either because they were very modern, as was the case with the 1970s steel roof over the Crimson Drawing Room, or because little or nothing remained after the fire. This phase led to the most important find of the first phase of the post-fire work at Windsor – the Great Kitchen Roof.

LEFT The roof of the Chester Tower being dismantled

BELOW Dismantling iron roof beams

DISCOVERIES

The Great Kitchen roof

The most striking feature of the Great Kitchen before the fire was its roof, with a great lantern stretching most of its length to provide daylight. However, it was thought that few, if any, remains of the early kitchen still survived in this part of the castle. There had been a kitchen on this site since the thirteenth century, but it was believed that the kitchen had been heavily rebuilt and re-roofed in the seventeenth century, and that Wyatville had replaced it in 1828, the date inscribed above a clock in the north wall.

The fire ran through this roof-space, charring the timbers and bringing down much of the plaster coving below the lantern, although most of the roof remained in place. Sections of the lantern had to be dismantled as they were too badly damaged to be safely left for repair. These were examined on the ground by our timber recorder, John Pidgeon, and he quickly noticed that the nineteenth-century softwood decorative detail was superficial, and had been nailed onto oak timbers of much earlier date.

Examination of the rest of the roof showed that the main structure was an early one, but until it could be dated accurately we had no idea how early it actually was, although we thought

that it might be fourteenth century. Given the potential importance of this discovery, it was quickly decided to conserve as much of the roof as possible, and to restore it rather than construct a replacement.

The intensive recording of this roof had two main aims. Firstly, to provide a full archaeological record of this structure (prior to this discovery, the earliest royal kitchen thought to have survived was that at Hampton Court Palace from the sixteenth century). The archaeological record was therefore of some importance in its own right. Secondly, it also had to provide the architects and engineers with an accurate survey and interpretation of the structure so that they could restore the roof, reinforcing it where necessary, without removing important evidence for the development and function of the structure.

The surviving timbers were grit-blasted to remove surface charring, and the roof was then restored. Old timbers were re-used wherever possible, but many of the lantern timbers were too badly burnt. New oak timbers were skilfully cut, replicating the techniques and joints used by the medieval carpenters, and the lantern was restored.

ABOVE Lantern truss being replaced in new timber

RIGHT General view of the kitchen roof as found after the fire

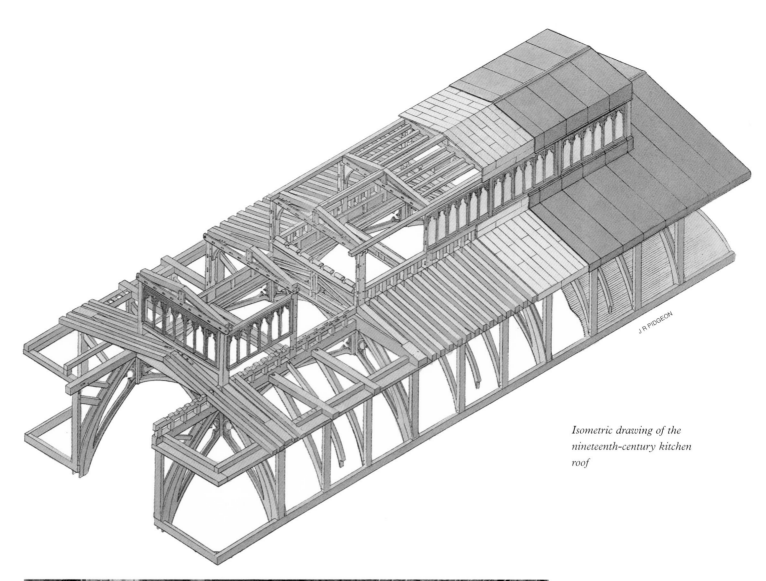

J R PIDGEON

Isometric drawing of the nineteenth-century kitchen roof

The same view of the kitchen roof after grit-blasting

15

The Kitchen roof and dendrochronology

Tree-ring dating, or 'dendrochronology' makes it possible to date timbers preserved in historic buildings and archaeological sites. Every year trees add a layer of new wood under the bark. Counting the rings on a freshly-felled tree gives the exact age of the tree. The date of historic timbers can be worked out by looking at the width of the rings, because the rings vary in width from year to year as a result of climate. Conditions favourable to growth result in a wide ring; unfavourable ones produce a narrow one. Trees of the same species growing at the same time show similar trends in tree-ring growth.

Tree-ring chronologies have been constructed by overlapping ring patterns from successively older samples. This has been done so that the record stretches back to 5000 BC. The tree-ring pattern from a timber of unknown date can then be compared to this master pattern, a process not unlike that of fingerprinting. When an acceptable match has been found, the date of each ring on the test sample can be read off. If the sample is complete, that is, if no wood has been lost from underneath the bark, then the date of the last ring will be the year in which the tree was felled. Oak is a tree ideally suited for tree-ring dating because it has very distinct rings. A quick polish with a sander reveals the boundaries of the rings. Oak also has a distinguishable band of sapwood. This is the outer part of a tree which transports the sap to the leaves. It is softer than the inner heartwood and is often recognisable in buildings because it is the only part of the timber which contains woodworm.

The first samples from the Great Kitchen were measured in 1993. Many were slices removed from fallen timbers during the initial clearing up process. Further samples were removed as cores from the timbers left standing. Initial indications suggested that there were at least two phases of timbers (see page 14), but as the restoration programme

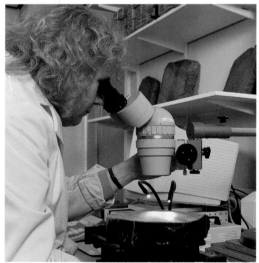

RIGHT A section of oak timber ready for measurement. Each growth ring is made up of spring wood (the light-coloured band) and summer wood (the dark-coloured band). Sapwood is present on the top right-hand corner of the sample and there are also one or two rings on the left edge

FAR RIGHT A slice of timber from the Kitchen being examined

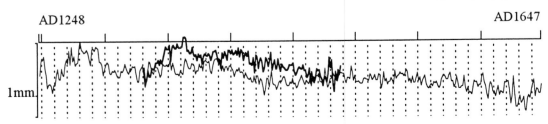

AD1248   AD1647

1mm

A graph showing the tree growth patterns for each year between 1248 and 1647

continued and more samples were obtained, the timbers began to tell an exciting story.

It was discovered that the kitchen roof contained timbers from at least four periods. Evidence for its medieval origin was given by the Truss I wallplate, which was felled some time after 1337. It was not possible to be more precise about the time of felling because there was no sapwood on the sample. There was also evidence from a cheek piece in Truss IV that the roof was altered in the eighteenth century. The bulk of the timbers, however, fell into two groups. One group was late fifteenth or early sixteenth century in date and the other was late sixteenth or early seventeenth century.

At first we thought we could be no more precise than this. The majority of the timbers were charred and had lost their sapwood. However, towards the end of the project we came across two samples, one from each group, which had complete sapwood. In the first, its last ring was incomplete, indicating that the tree had been felled in summer during its growing season. (If it had been a complete ring, the tree would have been felled in winter when it was dormant.) The outer ring dated to 1489. The other timber with complete sapwood, a wall piece in Truss X, was also felled in summer, but this time the year was 1577.

Research was done to link these findings with the documentary evidence. The fourteenth-century timber probably corresponds with Edward III's major rebuilding, as there is documentary evidence for work on the kitchen dating to 1362–63. In a list of urgently needed repairs of 1577, the kitchen roof was identified as a priority, to be 'searched and if neede be newe made'. Charges made in November 1577 include one for 'the Kytchen Roof'. It seems likely therefore that timbers were felled in summer 1577 and used almost immediately.

More puzzling was the date of 1489 for many of the timbers. The documentary sources reveal that various sums of money were paid to craftsmen between July 1489 and April 1490 to carry out some urgent repairs. The craftsmen included a carpenter, mason and a plumber (who worked with lead), and the purchase of lead is mentioned, suggesting repair work to a roof. Before the fire it was not known where these repairs were carried out. Dendrochronology identifies the roof in question as that of the Great Kitchen.

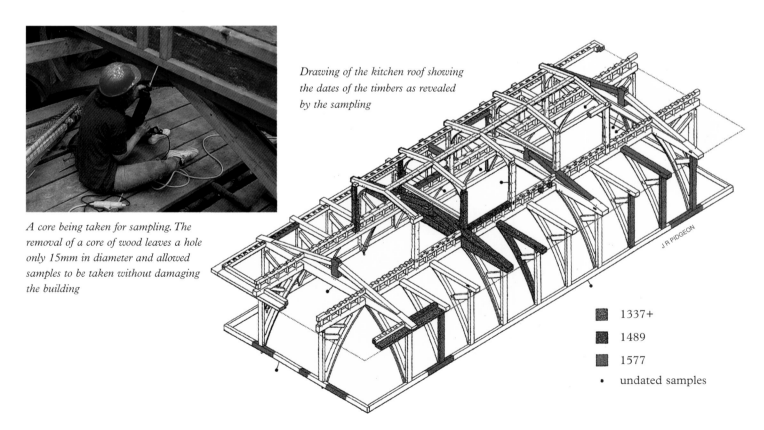

A core being taken for sampling. The removal of a core of wood leaves a hole only 15mm in diameter and allowed samples to be taken without damaging the building

Drawing of the kitchen roof showing the dates of the timbers as revealed by the sampling

J R PIDGEON

■ 1337+
■ 1489
■ 1577
• undated samples

The castle revealed

ABOVE A nineteenth-century window in a fourteenth-century window frame

RIGHT A fabric survey drawing of the east wall of the Kitchen Court showing the remodelling of windows and doors during different building phases

Once the buildings had been made safe, cleared, and the temporary roof was in position, what was left was a large masonry shell of enormous complexity. Our experience in the Round Tower had shown us that successive generations of builders had not replaced earlier buildings unless there was a pressing need to do so, either because the earlier buildings were unsafe, or because the new buildings had to be on a different alignment. As a result, many of the walls were earlier than had previously been thought, but had been altered many times since their construction. Wyatville had complained of this in 1830: '...many of the walls were cracked through, and many holes had been cut in, the Castle having been divided into different residences; it was very much dilapidated by each inhabitant cutting closets and cutting through walls without any regard to the destruction of it.' The processes of altering buildings in

successive generations had included the remodelling of doorways and windows, their blocking and replacement by new openings in different positions; the replacement of floors and roofs at different levels; the replacement of internal walls and wall linings, some of which left evidence cut into the main walls; and the expansion or extension of buildings so that former exterior wall surfaces were left enclosed within interior walls.

The successive waves of redevelopment since the late twelfth century had all left their mark

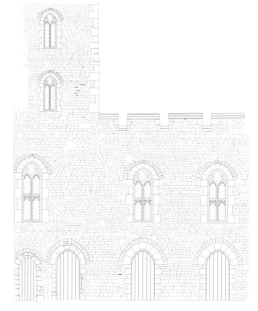

on the set of buildings, but it was very difficult to establish the date of much of this work. The features which might have helped to date the building phases – the form and decoration of doorways, windows and vaulting, the design of room interiors, and the timber floors and roofs inside the buildings – had almost all been removed and replaced in one building operation or another, and thus there was very little evidence left for the dating of the walls which we could see. We have therefore had to rely on our detailed record of the fabric of the buildings – the nature of the walling, and the relationships between different building phases – to arrive at an understanding of their development and form.

The other main reason for recording the building was to provide accurate measured survey drawings, and an interpretation of these drawings, for the architects and engineers working on the reconstruction project. The drawings which we produced were used by the project team in all stages of the reconstruction, from the marking-up of elevations for repairs and the installation of structural steelwork, to the production of new fabric wall-coverings and curtains. We have already seen how the archaeological information was critical to the reconstruction of the kitchen roof, but it was also essential to the repair of the medieval and later remains, minimising the disturbance caused by repair works.

It is also fair to say that some of the archaeological discoveries have influenced the design of the reconstruction project. A number of blocked doorways have been left re-opened, brought back into use after a gap of 150 years, or longer in some cases. A major restoration has been that of the fourteenth-century Kitchen Gate passage, formerly the main access to the kitchens from the Quadrangle, which was blocked in 1843. The largest such restoration was the opening-up of the vaults below St George's Hall, where a number of partition walls added between the seventeenth and nineteenth centuries were removed to reunite the long vaulted undercroft built in the 1360s. The drawings provided the basis of the reconstruction of missing elements of the vault, and will also serve as a record of the walls which had to be demolished. The following pages show how this drawn record was achieved.

Part of the medieval Undercroft after restoration

Blocked-up doorways and windows, such as this one in the Crimson Drawing Room, were revealed by the fire

LEFT *Reconstructions of the same wall as the drawing on page 18 as it may have appeared in the fourteenth century (top) and the seventeenth century (bottom)*

SURVEY TECHNIQUES

Hand survey, rectified photos & photogrammetry

Survey drawing of the Grand Reception Room ceiling

Accurate survey work is of vital importance, and it was not surprising that English Heritage's Survey Team were called to the castle within 48 hours of the 1992 fire to make an initial inspection of the devastated area. For this task we were able to draw on the valuable experience of recording fire-damaged buildings such as York Minster, the church of St Mary-at-Hill in the City of London, and Uppark in Sussex. The most striking initial impression was the sheer size of the area affected – something that had a major influence on planning.

There are a number of basic methods available when recording a historic building: chiefly hand and theodolite measurement, rectified photography and photogrammetry. Depending on the building involved, these can be used singly, or in combination. Collectively, they are known as Primary Measured Survey (PMS). At Windsor, several techniques were needed.

Traditional hand-drawn survey, using a tape-measure, spirit-level and plumb-line is a very labour-intensive method, but the simple equipment required and the direct contact with the fabric gives it several advantages. Where three-dimensional data on a large scale is needed, hand survey can be backed up by more sophisticated techniques and equipment, such as theodolite observations using EDM – Electro-magnetic Distance Measurers. However, at Windsor, the size of the problem meant that, while hand-survey would be useful in many areas, it could not possibly provide the whole solution.

Rectified photography and photogrammetry are two different techniques that use photographic images. Rectified photography is used where the surfaces to be recorded are largely flat. A photograph is taken precisely square-on to a flat elevation, and by placing some form of measured distance in the view, it is possible to produce a scaled photographic image. This can be used in its own right, or used as the basis for producing outline drawings, or joined together with other such rectified images to form a montage of an elevation (one such rectified photomontage, of an area of seventeenth-century wall-painting, is shown on page 53). This technique is obviously useful in many areas, but it is largely limited to flat, two-dimensional surfaces. Windsor presented much more complex surveying problems.

Photogrammetry is a survey technique that can be applied to any object – a landscape, a piece of furniture, or a building. The process relies on taking overlapping pairs of photographs (commonly known as 'stereo pairs') using a specialist 'metric' camera. Some form of scale is introduced into each stereo pair, usually by placing at least three small targets within the area of overlap and taking theodolite observations of them. This generates a series of measured co-ordinates and levels. The stereo-pair photographs can then be placed in a photogrammetric plotting machine, in which the two images can be read simultaneously as one 3-D image. A trained operator can trace over the outlines of this image to create a detailed survey drawing.

The uniqueness of photogrammetry is that the pair photographs capture images in three dimensions; this makes it particularly applicable to complex objects or surfaces. Furthermore, data can be directly transferred onto a computer file, rather than onto paper. This allows you to create a 3-D image, held digitally.

Photogrammetry is also very flexible: the data from numerous pair an be merged onto one file; the survey can be manipulated or added to; and it can be printed out on paper, to any scale.

The limitations of the use of photogrammetry are to do with access, working space and visibility. Virtually all the spaces to be recorded at Windsor were interiors. Many were cramped or complicated in shape, making it very difficult to take adequate stereo pair photographs. Furthermore, the site was soon bristling with scaffolding. The most difficult area was probably the Kitchen Court, where the complex plan and numerous cross walls made complete coverage difficult. In the end, it had to be tackled using a mixture of photogrammetry, rectified photography and hand survey. For this area alone 445 stereo pair photographs were taken.

We were greatly helped by the fact that a significant amount of measured survey work had been done before the fire. Stereo pair photographs of several of the State Apartments, including St George's Hall and the Grand Reception Room, had been commissioned and taken in 1985, but not plotted. In addition, accurate plans and cross-sections of the whole building had been made in 1986 by Sterling Surveys Ltd as preparation for a major re-wiring and servicing project; this provided vital 'as existed' information, and also a grid on which post-fire survey work could be based. Finally, after the Hampton Court fire in 1986, the Royal Household had commissioned rectified photography of the Private Apartments, including several rooms in the fire-damaged area. These were of less relevance to our archaeological work, but proved absolutely invaluable in planning the restoration of rooms such as the State Dining Room and the Crimson Drawing Room. All of this demonstrated conclusively the value of having accurate survey material, as an insurance against disaster.

Recorders undertaking survey work

Enhancement and interpretation

As we have seen, Primary Measured Survey (PMS), especially photogrammetry, was essential in producing a framework for the finished record drawings, as well as providing accurate images of the elevations which could be used immediately by the architects and engineers. The PMS was initially provided in hardcopy form at a scale of 1:20. This consisted of plotted photogrammetry and rectified photography, and digitally held data in a format that could be used by the Computer Aided Drafting (CAD) programme AutoCAD.

Where photogrammetry was available the data provided often had to be edited. There were often discrepancies between the plotting and the actual fabric due to the difficult nature of the site. This led to some detail being omitted as it was simply unclear on the original photographs themselves. Further detail was often exposed with the removal of panelling or plasterwork after photogrammetry had taken place, and this too had to be recorded. Information was also added which does not normally appear on such plots, notably features within the brickwork, and

The north wall of the Crimson Drawing Room: pre-fire rectified photograph

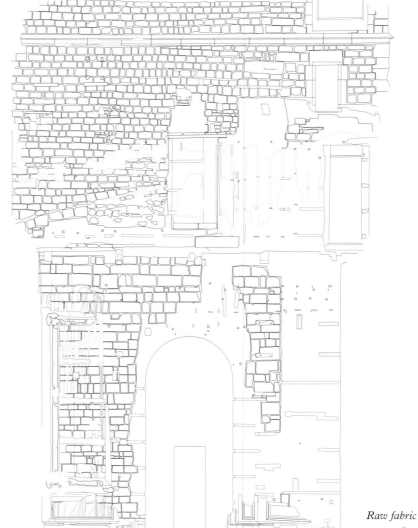

Raw fabric survey drawing

Post-fire rectified photograph

22

information on tooling (marks left by the preparation of the stone), pecking (hacking of the wall surface to provide a grip for plaster or render), masons' marks, graffiti, and ironwork embedded in the walls. This information was recorded by hand on site directly onto film overlays sitting on top of the 1:20 scale photogrammetric plot. This new information was then added to the digital photogrammetric drawing by a technique known as digitising.

Rectified photography and hand survey were used where photogrammetry was not appropriate. This information also had to be transposed into a digital drawing readable in CAD. To produce digital drawings from the hand survey was simply a matter of initially digitising the hand-measured drawings, then using survey control from observed targets to slot the drawings into the three-dimensional site grid. Use of the rectified photographs, however, involved a two-stage process. Firstly, information was digitised directly from the photographs themselves and located within the site grid in the same way as with the hand survey. Secondly, these drawings were then plotted out and edited on site, as with the PMS material, with any additional information gathered being digitised into the original digital drawing.

The resulting highly accurate record allows us to model rooms and buildings in three dimensions. This will be of enormous benefit in analysis, both in understanding how the buildings worked and in the presentation of reconstructions and models.

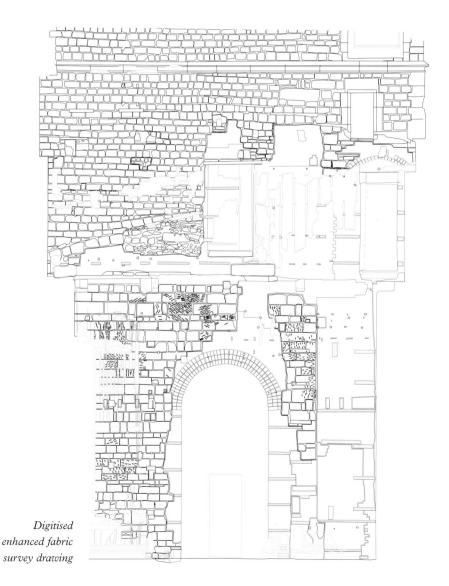

Digitised enhanced fabric survey drawing

Undertaking hand survey to add details to PMS

Adding details to digital drawings held on computer

Excavations and finds

A gold coin of Edward IV found in the Undercroft (see page 51)

Recent excavation at Windsor has largely been 'rescue' archaeology – we have only excavated in those areas where the buried remains were in danger of damage or destruction by engineering and other construction works. In the Round Tower, large-scale excavation was necessary as much of the surface of the motte was going to be destroyed in the underpinning operation. The excavation work in the Upper Ward was much more limited in scope, as the reconstruction of the fire-damaged buildings involved relatively little below-ground work. However, new foundations had to be laid out in the Kitchen Court area, and drains had to be renewed throughout the area, and so there was some opportunity to find out what survived below the surface.

One of the problems in planning excavations at Windsor was that we had no idea of what we were likely to find; these sites had not been excavated before, and it was not known what might have survived. The first step in each case was therefore evaluation – the excavation of trial trenches to discover what survived below the surface. In most cases, we found that good archaeological remains did survive, but that they were very fragile – close to the surface and thus vulnerable to the various redevelopments. They had also been badly damaged in the past; the digging of trenches for drains and other services had removed much of the archaeology, as had the construction of foundations for modern buildings.

Drawing of the Kitchen Court wall foundations

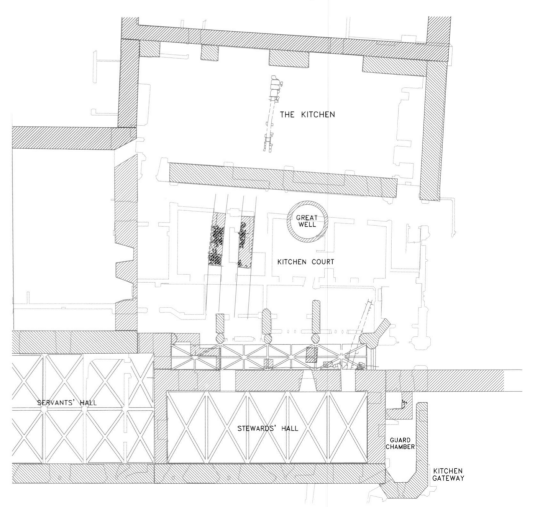

▨ 12th century
▨ 13th century
▨ 14th century
☐ post 14th century

Once the decision was taken to excavate, the areas were opened up. All excavation has been by hand, using a variety of tools depending on what had to be removed – from trowels and brushes to picks, shovels and jack-hammers. We were looking for a variety of evidence: building foundations, floors and construction deposits, drains, pits and rubbish layers. It was also very useful to examine the buried foundations of the standing buildings, as in many cases these were found to incorporate earlier structures and materials. The best-preserved remains were found inside the Round Tower, where we excavated a sequence of kitchen floors and hearths dating from the late twelfth century to the middle of the fourteenth century. These layers contained a great deal of broken pottery, which will help us to date the sequence as well as informing us about cooking practices. The kitchen floors also contained large quantities of animal bone – cow, pig, sheep, deer, and a very wide variety of birds and fish – which will help us to understand the diet of the occupants of the castle.

In the Upper Ward, we found a great deal of evidence for drainage, including a number of cess-pits. All of the stone-lined cess-pits had been cleaned out during the medieval period, and all we found was the rubble used to backfill them when they went out of use. We did find one early (possibly twelfth-century) cess-pit which contained a very wide variety of animal and plant remains; and these can be compared with the excavated kitchen remains to tell us a great deal about food preparation and consumption.

Over the last few pages we have described the methodologies used by the archaeologists in our work at Windsor. We will now look at a number of examples which show how these techniques have combined to create our new understanding of the development of parts of the castle.

Excavation in progress in the Kitchen Court showing (left) the seventeenth-century access steps to the well; and (right) medieval foundations in front of the seventeenth-century New Kitchen

COMBINING THE EVIDENCE

The Kitchen sequence

Cross-section through the Kitchen, showing how it was built against the twelfth-century curtain wall

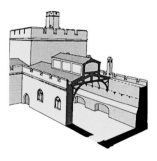

Isometric cut-away view of the Kitchen after its fourteenth-century remodelling

The earliest-known view of the castle, dating from about 1450, showing the kitchen roof-lantern (bottom left-hand corner of the castle)

The Great Kitchen at Windsor is one of the oldest continuously used kitchens in the country. Yet its antiquity has become clear only recently; Sir William Hope, in his great study of the castle (1913), believed most of it to be a rebuilding from the late seventeenth century. The 1992 fire revealed the historic oak roof behind the decorative nineteenth-century casing (see page 14), and then the removal of thick layers of plaster from the walls laid bare its complex earlier history.

The north wall of the Kitchen is, in fact, the twelfth-century stone curtain wall, with great medieval fireplaces (unused since the 1820s) set against it. When the plaster was cut away, the backs of the fireplaces were found to be the very hard Bagshot Heath stone used at the castle for facing external walls; this strongly suggests that in the 1170s there was no permanent building here, just the curtain wall. The next strand in the evidence, chronologically, is a fine stone drain found beneath the floor, sloping away to the north. It is hard to date with certainty, but is early.

At some point during the thirteenth century, a great stone kitchen building was built here, behind the curtain wall; references in the building accounts for 1259 for construction of 'the Queen's Kitchen' may refer to this spot. No masonry, however, can definitely be identified as of this period, but a blocked doorway in the south-west corner of the present Kitchen leads through to the site of the thirteenth-century Great Hall.

The Kitchen was constructed in approximately its present form during Edward III's great rebuilding between 1357 and 1377. The curtain wall was thickened to provide fireplaces, and carried on up; the sloping section of the wall represents where it is set back, above the twelfth-century curtain wall (see cross-section). The south wall was rebuilt with three big pointed windows, and a great timber roof added with a top lantern for light and ventilation. The earliest known view of the castle, from a manuscript history of England in the library of Eton College, shows the Kitchen with a lantern on its roof. The roof, however, must have decayed badly over the next century, for as we have seen it was largely reconstructed in 1489, probably following the fourteenth-century design quite closely.

During Hugh May's work for Charles II, the Kitchen was modernised, the windows re-cut to a rectangular shape, and the walls patched with red brickwork. Soon after this, it seems, the great room was regarded as obsolete, and a new kitchen built to the south in the Kitchen Court (the dating of this is not clear, but the red brick used is of a different size to that used in the Kitchen proper, making it unlikely that these developments are of the same date). In a plan of about 1740, the great medieval kitchen is subdivided into six compartments.

Wyatville restored the great room to its primacy as the heart of the royal kitchens, as it has remained ever since. He added the large new fireplaces and chimney-stacks at the east and west ends, which still retain their spectacular iron grates and ranges. Wyatville's massive Gothic kitchen tables and work-benches all survive, as do the shelves around the room, with long brass strips bearing numbers for the legion of brass and copper kitchen implements which are kept here. Thus, the Royal Kitchen, as well as being revealed as a medieval building of exceptional interest, also has one of the best-preserved ensembles of nineteenth-century kitchen fittings.

ETON COLLEGE

LEFT *Fabric survey drawing of the south elevation of the Kitchen, showing the windows as remodelled in the seventeenth and nineteenth centuries* BELOW *A watercolour of the Royal Kitchen, c.1819, by James Stephanoff for Pyne's* Royal Residences. *There has never, in fact, been a stone vault over this room; the ceiling may have been painted to resemble stonework*

The Grand Reception Room

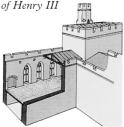

Tower and hall, at the time of Henry III

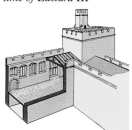

Great Chamber, at the time of Edward III

Great Watching Chamber, at the time of Edward IV

Guard Chamber, at the time of Charles II

Grand Reception Room, at the time of George IV

Historical sequence, showing the development of the Grand Reception Room

OPPOSITE *The Grand Reception Room before the fire*

The Upper Ward buildings reach a peak of complexity in the Grand Reception Room. During the 1992 fire, its splendid 1820s plaster ceiling was destroyed, but the elaborate panelling remained largely undamaged. In order to speed up the drying-out of the fabric, it was necessary to remove the great backing-boards for the tapestries and mirrors. This made twelve large 'windows' through the panelling, through which some of the room's complex building history could be seen. Much more evidence came from the general stripping of surfaces in the rooms below the Grand Reception Room: the Pastry Kitchen, Dry Goods Store and various passageways.

The first *Domus Regis*, probably built in the early twelfth century for Henry I, seems to have been a square quadrangular building, with towers at its north-west and north-east corners. The Grand Reception Room represents the site of the north-east tower and the east range, but all we know of this early period is from evidence in the foundations.

Far more positive evidence emerges for the thirteenth century. Features found in the ground-floor rooms strongly suggest that this was Henry III's private hall (as opposed to the other hall in the Lower Ward for more public entertaining). Deep window embrasures in the Dry Goods Store turned out to be very early, with one retaining a stone window-seat and the sill of a large window, clearly indicating that here was a room of high status. In the neighbouring Pastry Kitchen, areas of fine lining-masonry and a wide blocked doorway to the Kitchen appeared. Next, we found a major blocked doorway with thirteenth-century mouldings from what had been the central Cloister Court, immediately opposite the door into the Kitchen. Putting this together allowed us to make a conjectural reconstruction of a small but finely detailed hall. This lasted little over a century, until Edward III's remodelling.

Around 1360, Henry's hall was half-demolished, its roof and upper walls completely removed. A new Great Chamber was then built above it at first floor level; the ground-floor

rooms thus created have been used as kitchen areas ever since. In the south-west corner of the new Chamber was a huge entrance door with a three-centred arch, rediscovered behind the panelling.

The rooms seems to have been remodelled again about a century later. The evidence for this is a pair of blocked window openings with segmental arches, immediately above the blocked door but evidently not contemporary with it. The spacing of the arches implies a series of close-spaced windows at high level, like those in the halls at Eltham Palace (1475), or Hampton Court (c.1529–31). This may well tie in with a reference in the accounts for 1477–78, to the roof and 'silyng' of Edward IV's Great Chamber being reconstructed.

Yet further radical remodelling was carried out by Hugh May for Charles II, c.1674–80. May wanted to make a great new Guard Chamber here, and to give it a commanding view over the North Terrace. He tore down the twelfth-century tower at its north end to extend the room northwards – a wall scar shows where the tower was – and demolished and rebuilt the east wall in order to create two huge new windows there, looking over the Kitchen Court. The rebuilt room was decorated by Antonio Verrio, and magnificently fitted with a display of weapons by John Harris, Master-Armourer at the Tower of London, whose designs for the layout still survive in the Royal Armouries.

James Wyatt, 're-gothicising' the castle for George III in 1800, built a square extension to the room northwards overlooking the North Terrace. This was named the Blenheim Tower, but it proved very short-lived, as Wyatt's nephew Jeffry Wyatville demolished it and carried out the last great remodelling, to create the present Grand Reception Room. He raised the parapet by about 2 metres to improve the skyline, and named the result the Cornwall Tower. Inside, the splendid panelling and plasterwork, one of the greatest set-pieces of Regency decoration, were installed, and the room's complex archaeology disappeared again for over 160 years.

The Chester Tower & Crimson Drawing Room

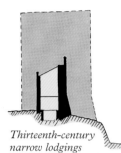

Twelfth-century curtain wall

Thirteenth-century narrow lodgings

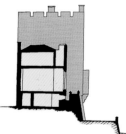

Fourteenth-century lodging range

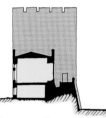

Seventeenth-century remodelling

After nineteenth-century remodelling

Historical sequence of reconstructions, showing the development of the lodging range

The fire burnt out the Crimson Drawing Room and damaged the Chester Tower, where it was eventually stopped. In the fourteenth century these areas were not in the palace proper, but were part of the long, narrow lodging ranges which lined the south and east sides of the Upper Ward, providing accommodation for the royal family and the court.

Windsor seems to have been one of the first places to have lodging ranges of this type. Their general form is well known, and survives today at places such as Dartington Hall, Devon (*c.*1386), St Cross Hospital, Winchester (*c.*1445), Hampton Court Palace (*c.*1515), and in several Oxford and Cambridge colleges of the fourteenth to seven-teenth centuries. Nowhere, though, were lodgings planned on quite so grand a scale as here.

The post-fire investigations have allowed us to piece together the history of the eastern range with some confidence. In the 1170s, Henry II built the first stone defences around the Upper Ward. Some of this masonry survives at low level. When first built, the Chester Tower was simply an 'open-gorged' tower – without a rear wall – comparable to contemporary towers, for instance at Framlingham in Suffolk (1190–1210), or at Dover, remodelled by Henry II *c.*1168–85. It seems likely that most of the Upper Ward towers, when first built, were of this type.

In the thirteenth century the Chester Tower was enclosed with solid rear walls. About the same time a lodging range was built up against the curtain wall to its north; we found its foundations, and a large chalk-lined 'garderobe' or latrine pit. As we have not excavated to the south of the Tower, we cannot be sure if the

same happened in that direction, though this seems likely.

The definitive rebuilding, here as elsewhere, came with Edward III's work in the 1360s. The thirteenth-century range was demolished, and new, much larger lodgings built, up to the line of the Tower. The 1992 fire destroyed the Crimson Drawing Room's ceiling and panelling and revealing striking new evidence, notably the fourteenth-century roofline, and remains of two very large blocked window openings which once looked onto the Kitchen Court. On the ground floor of the Chester Tower, large fitted cupboards were removed, revealing much lining-masonry, an arched doorway, and part of a fine medieval fireplace; we are unclear whether this is thirteenth- or fourteenth-century work.

The range became progressively grander with each successive rebuilding. Hugh May, remodelling the castle for Charles II, wanted to make the rooms look outwards, and in order to create large arched windows he demolished much of the medieval curtain wall at principal-floor level. Equally dramatically, he constructed a great new terrace along the east front, with its feet in the medieval dry moat.

After May's rebuilding, the east front continued to be occupied by relatively small lodgings for the royal family and court. The last stage of remodelling came with George IV, who wanted to create new private apartments for himself there. The king demanded altogether larger rooms, and Wyatville was obliged to make drastic structural interventions to create the splendid suite of White, Green and Crimson Drawing Rooms.

Wyatville demolished the Chester Tower above first-floor level and rebuilt it, in order to accommodate the Green Drawing Room. He cut a huge hole into the curtain wall to make the new Crimson Drawing Room's bay window, and added an extra storey on top. Sumptuous panelling and decoration, much of it salvaged from Carlton House on Pall Mall, was installed, making these rooms one of the finest set-pieces of Regency taste in Britain.

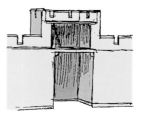

Twelfth–century

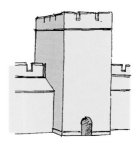

Thirteenth–century

Fourteenth–century

Historical sequence of reconstructions of the Chester Tower

ABOVE *A fourteenth-century window arch, found behind panelling in the Crimson Drawing Room*

LEFT *Morel & Seddon's design for the Crimson Drawing Room, 1826*

THE EARLY CASTLE

Windsor 1066–1216

Plan of the early 'King's House' in the Upper Ward

An imaginative reconstruction drawing by Terry Ball of the early castle during the siege of 1216

Windsor Castle is thought to have been founded by the William the Conqueror in the early years of his reign, around 1070, but there is no firm evidence for its existence until 1086 when it is mentioned in the Domesday survey. The earliest castle was built of earth and timber, with banks of chalk rubble quarried from the castle ditches topped with timber palisades, and dominated by the large man-made mound or 'motte' which divided the Upper and Lower Wards. The early castle was not the main royal residence in the area; until the early twelfth century, kings continued to use Edward the Confessor's palace at Old Windsor. By 1110, however, Henry I was holding his Easter court at the castle, and ever since then it has been one of the most important royal residences.

The motte was the key element in the early defences, and it is here that the best evidence has been found for the eleventh- to thirteenth-century development of the castle. In its earliest phase, the motte was ringed by a timber palisade, traces of which were found in excavation. There was probably a central timber tower, similar to examples found on other sites, but this part of the motte summit has been destroyed by later events. The surface of the motte was covered by a thin ashy deposit

containing animal bones, representing occupation, but there were no remains of other buildings on the summit. There is, however, evidence for a well in the north-western part of the summit. This occupation came to a sudden end with the catastrophic collapse of a large part of the motte; the southern half of the summit slumped by over 2 metres.

The summit of the motte was quickly repaired, levelled up with a thick layer of chalk rubble and stabilised with timber piles driven deep into the body of the motte. The medieval builders clearly had great confidence in this solution as they then built the first stone defences around its summit. Only the foundation of this first shell-keep has been found, consisting of a sloping plinth of flint rubble. There may have been a projecting tower to the north-east, possibly the entrance, and the first well was replaced by a new stone-lined well. Internal

buildings were of timber, set into shallow trenches or beam-slots. There were a number of large pits in the eastern part of the summit, one of which was timber-lined, but it is not known what these were for. At a slightly later date large buttress foundations were added to the keep; as these were of chalk, it is unlikely that they were designed to hold the walls up, so it is perhaps more likely that they were an architectural embellishment. The foundations of a second defensive wall or 'chemise' seem to have been added to the first tower while it was still standing.

The first keep seems to have continued to suffer from subsidence; the stonework showed clear signs of cracking, with the worst effects around the weak southern half of the summit. The problem was solved by the construction of the second shell keep inside the line of the first; the foundation of this keep is quite shallow around the northern edge, and barely wider than the wall itself, but to the south it was given a much more massive foundation, 4 metres wide and 2 metres deep, and the wall line was pulled back from the edge of the motte summit to give the tower its characteristic 'squashed' plan. This keep is thought to have been built in the late twelfth century, part of the work of Henry II who is thought to have built the masonry defences of the Upper Ward and part of the Lower Ward. Some evidence for this has been found in the Upper Ward for the curtain wall and the projecting rectangular towers, and it is possible that the basic layout of the King's House was formed in this period. It was in this state, with the castle defences still not completed in stone, that Windsor successfully withstood a prolonged siege in 1216 by the forces opposed to King John.

The dating of all of this is very problematic. If we accept that the present tower was built in the late twelfth century, then there was a great deal of activity in the first hundred years of the castle's life. It is just possible that the surviving shell keep is later, dating from the repair of the 'houses in the mount' in 1227 following damage sustained in the siege of 1216, but this seems unlikely on stylistic grounds – it looks like a twelfth-century shell keep. This is one of the questions which might be answered by the detailed analysis of the finds and structural sequence.

Excavating the well in the Round Tower

Remains of the first shell keep and the pilaster buttresses added to it

Excavating the earliest floor surface in the Round Tower, dating from the late eleventh century

The reign of Henry III

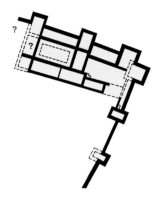

Plan of the Upper Ward after Henry III's rebuilding

A thirteenth-century external wall, now enclosed

Cusp-headed window in the Steward's Hall

In 1216 King John died, and was succeeded by his nine-year old son, Henry; in the same year England was invaded by a French army under the Dauphin Louis. Windsor faced the supreme test of a three-month siege by a French army under the Comte de Nevers. The castle held out under its castellan, Engelard de Cigogne, in spite of the fact that part of its defences were still only in earth and wood. In 1221 de Cigogne was authorised to spend money rebuilding a wall damaged during the siege, and this was followed by a whole series of payments for works in the castle, including repairs to the 'king's house' in the Upper Ward. The Henry III Tower at the corner of the Middle Ward and the so-called Edward III Tower at the south-west corner of the Upper Ward probably date from these years, as does the wall closing the west end of the Lower Ward with its three great drum towers. This completed the circuit of the castle's outer walls.

In 1227 Henry III came of age; and reigned until 1272. He owned almost sixty royal castles, of which Windsor was already the largest, and it became one of his favourite residences, alongside the Palace of Westminster and Clarendon Palace in Wiltshire. Although his reign was politically chaotic, Henry was one of the greatest builders and patrons of the arts ever to sit on the English throne, and he is chiefly remembered for his rebuilding of Westminster Abbey. After his marriage to Eleanor of Provence in 1236, he began a series of building campaigns at Windsor, remodelling the 'king's house' in the Upper Ward, and the royal apartments in the Lower Ward. By 1260 he had spent over £10,000 on Windsor.

The Lower Ward seems to have housed the garrison. There was also a Great Hall, just north of where St George's Chapel now stands. From 1240, Henry added several more buildings; a chamber for himself, a chamber for the queen and a chapel, around a small courtyard. A part of these buildings survive, though much altered, as the present Dean's Cloister, and some of their thirteenth-century detail remains, as does a magnificent door at the east end of St George's Chapel; these still give one an idea of the style and quality of Henry's work.

In the Upper Ward Henry remodelled and added to the *Domus Regis* or 'king's house' over a twenty-year period. Until the 1992 fire, nothing was firmly known about his work here, apart from the rather cryptic entries in the Exchequer and Liberate Rolls. The archaeological investigations since then have provided many more clues, and we can now tentatively identify several walls, surfaces and features as thirteenth century, though we are far from having the whole picture. It is particularly difficult to distinguish between the twelfth-century palace which Henry III found, and his additions.

Like Westminster and Clarendon, Henry III's palace at Windsor was informal and asymmetrical in its planning. The courtyard in the middle, the area now occupied by the Waterloo Chamber, seems to have been the 'spicerye garden' referred to in the documents – it was planted as a herb garden. References to the 'king's cloister' suggest it may have been surrounded by cloister walks. On the east side, on the site of the Grand Reception Room, there was a hall at ground floor level, for which we have found evidence (see above, page 28).

Further east, in the present Kitchen Court, Henry built a kitchen. To the south there was a range of buildings on the site of St George's Hall, with a major room at upper-floor level. At the west end of this (the site of the State Entrance) there was a higher building, perhaps a tower forming the principal entrance. At the east end, Henry added a narrower range, represented by the present Steward's Hall. Of the details and interiors, only tantalising fragments remain. A fireplace, probably from his reign, emerged from behind panelling in St George's Hall. A fine cusped-headed window, blocked for several centuries, was discovered in the Steward's Hall, and two nearby doors can be identified as belonging to his reign. Most of the decorative detail of the thirteenth-century palace, though, was swept away in the following century, by Edward III.

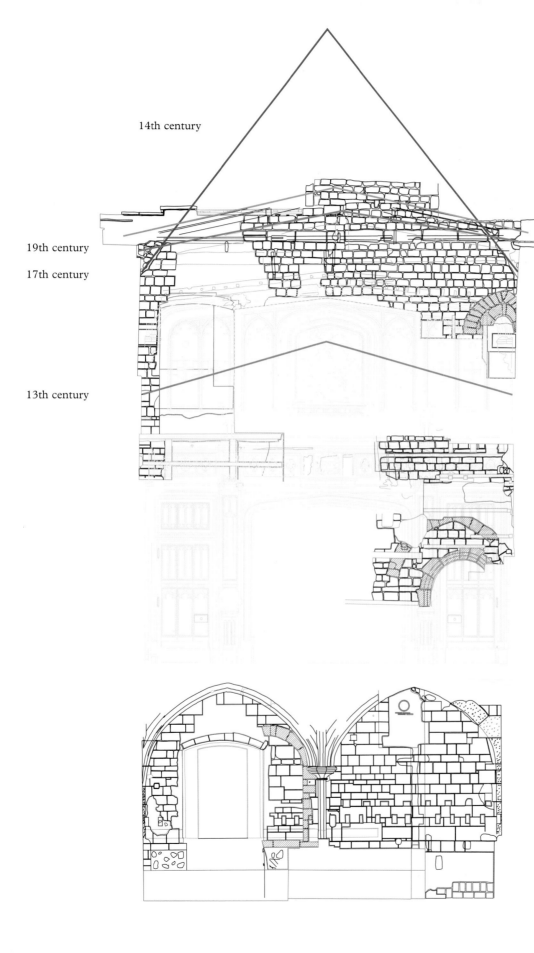

14th century

19th century

17th century

13th century

Fabric survey drawing of the west end of St George's Hall. The removal of nineteenth-century plasterwork revealed that this wall consisted of thirteenth-century masonry for most of its height. Furthermore, it holds valuable evidence of the medieval rooflines. These are (starting with the lowest) of the thirteenth century, the seventeenth century, the nineteenth century and finally the steeply-pitched fourteenth-century roofline (see page 37). Note the blocked arch leading onto the thirteenth-century roof level

The restored undercroft

The long expanse of St George's Hall, the largest state-room in any British royal palace, is the architectural and ceremonial heart of the castle. Since the time of Henry III or earlier, there has been a succession of great state-rooms here. Yet until the fire, all that one could see was Wyatville's lath-and-plaster surfaces of the 1820s. The fire, burning away these layers, revealed the complex history of this range for the first time in 170 years.

In the twelfth century, under Henry I and Henry II, the 'Kings House' was a compact, square quadrangular block, its long south side where St George's Hall now is, although the only evidence we have from this early period is at foundation level.

However, we now have valuable new evidence from the reign of Henry III. At the west end of St George's Hall, the cutting-away of damaged plaster revealed a series of historic rooflines and much other evidence – we were looking at a thirteenth-century wall, standing to over 16 metres (50 feet) in height! This told us that Henry III built a two-storey building here, with a low-pitched (and probably battlemented)

roof; it abutted against a high tower where the State Entrance now is, and a little doorway led out from the tower onto the roof. Blocked, early doorways revealed that the thirteenth-century floor heights were at about the present levels. We are still not sure what this new room was – perhaps the king's own chamber, or perhaps his chapel. Further east, Henry III added another chamber of the same width, of which we found the fireplace (hidden behind nineteenth-century panelling). Even further east, he added a narrower range, represented by the ground-floor room known as the Steward's Hall.

Edward III demanded that every element of the palace become larger and more splendid. He ruthlessly remodelled this range to make a great new hall and chapel at principal floor level. On the ground floor a long vaulted undercroft, comparable to that of a great monastery, was built. This survives in its entirety, preserving the eighteen-bay rhythm of the fourteenth-century building. Above this were the immense hall and chapel, marked out by their steeply pitched roofs (55 degrees, when most of the roofs of Windsor were about 17 degrees).

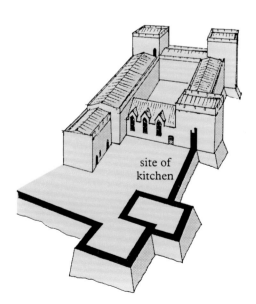

site of kitchen

Historical sequence drawings:
Henry III's buildings (thirteenth century)

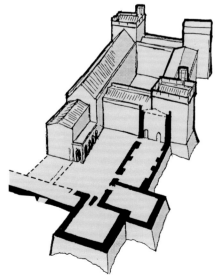

Fourteenth century Phase I:
hall and chapel

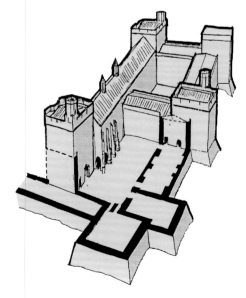

Fourteenth century Phase II:
extended hall and chapel with buttressed arcade

Enigmatic evidence has appeared that the substantial fourteenth-century rebuilding happened in two phases; a first phase creating a hall and chapel range thirteen bays long, and a second phase extending it eastwards for another five bays over the Steward's Hall and the 'Larderie Passage' arcade. Buttresses were added to the arcade, to enable it to support the massive additional weight of the extended hall. We are not yet clear why this might have been. There is no doubt, however, of the grandeur of the new building, housing the largest royal hall in England after Westminster. The hall's appearance is known from one engraving by Wenceslas Hollar, showing its magnificent timber roof, probably by the master-carpenter William Herland. Another two surviving drawings by Hollar show the neighbouring Chapel, shortly before it was remodelled in the 1670s, as Windsor was re-invented again for Charles II.

Engraving by Wenceslas Hollar of Charles II holding the Garter Feast in the medieval St George's Hall, c.1668

THE CASTLE'S GLORY
Edward III's rebuilding

Under Edward III (reigned 1328–77), Windsor reached the height of its glory as the pre-eminent residence of the kings of England, rivalling the palace of Westminster itself. Edward's work at Windsor has to be understood within the context of his victories in the Hundred Years War, the cult of chivalry, and the foundation of the Order of the Garter.
Edward was a victorious warrior king. During his reign England was devastated by the Black

Death, but this did not prevent him from re-launching the Plantagenet dynasty's ambitions to dominate France – claiming the throne of France itself through his mother Isabella, daughter of the last of the old Capetian kings. A succession of victories, notably at Crécy (1346), the capture of Calais (1347) and Poitiers (1356), delivered a large part of France into his hands. The English took hordes of noble captives – the kings of France and Scotland

Bird's-eye view of Windsor Castle, c.1658, by Wenceslas Hollar

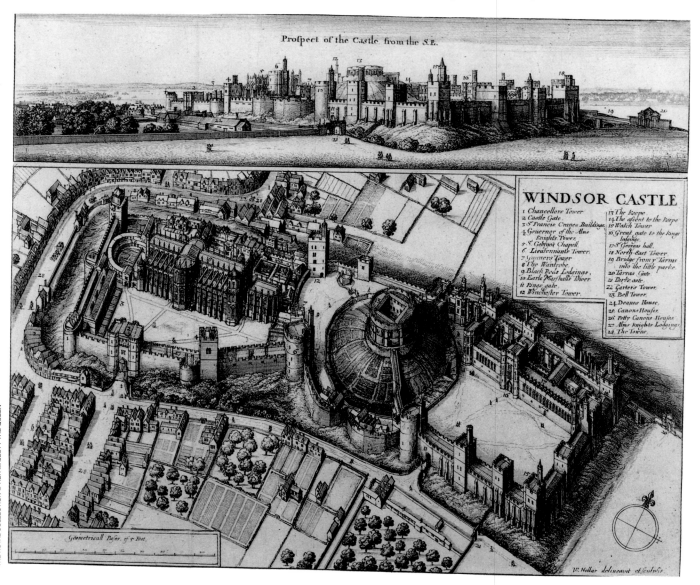

Prospect of the Castle from the S.E.

WINDSOR CASTLE

1 Chancellors Tower
2 Castle Gate
3 S.t Frances Cranes Buildings
4 Gouernor of the Alms Knights Tower
5 S.t Georges Chappell
6 Lieutennants Tower
7 Gunners Tower
8 The Wardrybe
9 Black Rods Lodgings
10 Earle Marshalls Tower
11 Kings gate
12 Winchester Tower
13 The Keepe
14 The ascent to the Keepe
15 Watch Tower
16 Great gate to the Kings lodgings
17 S.t Georges hall
18 North-East Tower
19 Bridge from y.e Tarras into the little parke
20 Tarras Gate
21 Darke gate
22 Garters Tower
23 Bell Tower
24 Deanes House
25 Canons House
26 Petty Canons House
27 Alms knights Lodgings
28 The Towne

Geometricall Paßes of 5 Feet.

V. Hollar delineauit et sculpsit

were both Edward's prisoners at various times – and the scale of the ransoms paid goes some way to explaining the scale and grandeur of Edward's buildings.

Military success helped breed a new cult of chivalry at Edward's court; tournaments, which had previously been a relatively straightforward combination of sport and military training, were becoming overlaid with a new romantic view of knighthood. In January 1344, Edward held a great tournament at Windsor, at which he announced the foundation of a new order of the Round Table, also that he would erect a 'most noble building' at Windsor, to house its meetings. From the accounts it is clear that a good deal of work was done in the summer of 1344, but the project was then abandoned. No trace of this mysterious building has ever been found, and in the event the king instead founded the Order of the Garter in 1348, which remains the world's oldest order of chivalry.

From the first, the Order of the Garter was based at Windsor, and the king founded a new collegiate church dedicated to St George to serve as its chapel. He gave the thirteenth-century chapel and hall in the Lower Ward built by his great-grandfather Henry III to his new foundation, and the College of St George – comprising the Dean and Canons – has lived there ever since.

From 1357 until his death in 1377 Edward was continuously engaged in the rebuilding of Windsor. It was a vast job, eventually costing around £50,000 – representing the most expensive secular building project of the entire Middle Ages in England. The Black Death had left England short of skilled labour, and all over the country the king's sheriffs had to coerce masons and carpenters into going to work at Windsor.

The rebuilding started with the remodelling of the Round Tower. A new timber-framed building was fitted into the twelfth-century stone shell, housing a royal residence in miniature with a hall, a kitchen, royal chambers, and a well. It may be that this was deliberately planned as a temporary residence, for the king's use while work was proceeding in the Upper Ward. Much of the fourteenth-century work in the Round Tower survives, and was revealed and recorded in 1989–92.

Thereafter, the Upper Ward buildings were remodelled, the builders working clockwise from the (mis-named) Norman Gate at the north-west corner, around to the Edward III Tower at the south-west corner. It was not, apparently, the king's primary aim to strengthen Windsor's defences – the twelfth-century curtain walls remained largely as they were, although walls and towers may have been raised, to provide more accommodation and to enhance the skyline.

The south and east sides of the Upper Ward were lined with two-storey lodgings for the court. On the north side, Edward remodelled and extended Henry III's palace, creating a huge complex around three courtyards. By 1377 Windsor was the largest palace in England, a building to rival anything on the continent. Edward's work has remained the matrix for the development of the castle ever since, and for all the many later alterations, the outlines of his plan can still be made out.

In the mid seventeenth century, the Czech artist Wenceslas Hollar made a series of views of Windsor, commissioned by the antiquary Elias Ashmole as illustrations for his *History and Institutions of the Order of the Garter* (1672). When the views are examined in detail, anomalies and mistakes start to appear. Nevertheless, Hollar's beautiful drawings and engravings are absolutely invaluable, and are by far the best record we have of the Plantagenet castle. They give a palpable sense of Windsor just before its Baroque remodelling, and largely as Edward III had left it, a great fortified citadel rising above the town and the wooded parks like something out of a Book of Hours.

A survey reconstruction drawing by John Pidgeon of the fourteenth-century timber-framed lodgings in the Round Tower

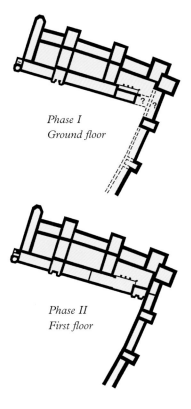

Phase I Ground floor

Phase II First floor

Plans of the Upper Ward in the fourteenth century

Windsor and the Perpendicular style

Edward III's work at Windsor represented a crucial phase in the development of the English Perpendicular style – one of the most distinctive English contributions to European architecture. The key figure in the work at Windsor was probably the king's Clerk of Works, William of Wykeham, later Bishop of Winchester and Chancellor of England. Ranulf Higden, author of a contemporary chronicle, the *Polychronicon Anglorum*, said that 'considering how he could please the King and secure his goodwill, he counselled the King to build the said Castle of Windsor in such wise as appears today'. William of Wykeham later employed the same master mason, William Wynford, to build his two foundations, Winchester College and New College, Oxford. There are many points of similarity, and the latter are probably the best places to gauge the architectural style and effect of Edward III's Windsor.

The rebuilt castle was grand, but severe and restrained, the external walls faced in the very hard-wearing Bagshot Heath stone. It turns out that the flint 'galletting' in the joints, always thought to be medieval, was only introduced in the late seventeenth-century works, probably for self-consciously picturesque reasons. The core of the thick walls is in chalk/clunch rubble. The internal walls were lined with fine ashlar masonry in clunch or chalk – soft, and so easy to cut. The finer elements, such as arches, door and window surrounds and vault ribs – were often in greensand stones, such as Reigate stone from Surrey (found in many royal buildings of the Middle Ages).

The focus of the great building was the long hall-chapel range, discussed above (pages 36–37). The immensely long eighteen-bay range was marked out by having a steep-pitched (55 degree) roof, whereas the remainder of the buildings had low-pitched roofs concealed behind their battlements. To offset the horizontal stress of the long row of windows, the facade was dramatically framed by two great vertical accents – a pair of very tall identical gatehouse towers, known as the Spicerie Gate (on the site

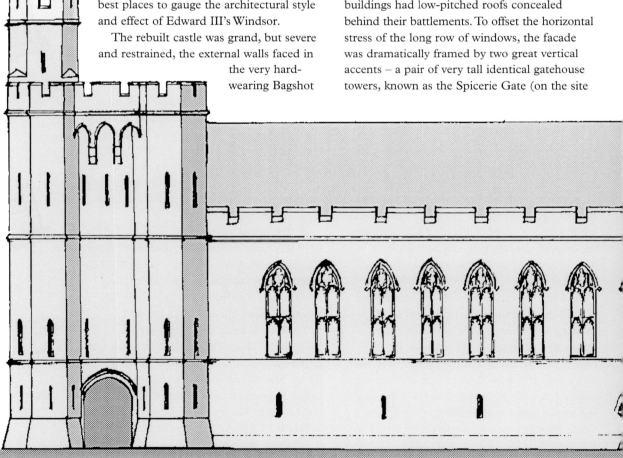

A reconstruction drawing of Edward III's imposing hall, chapel, and flanking gatehouses

of the State Entrance) and the Kitchen Gate (on the site of the Equerries' Entrance). They had slightly canted turrets, with machicolations (projecting battlements) carried across between the turrets, similar to the surviving gatehouse at Carisbrooke Castle on the Isle of Wight, another royal work of *c*.1380.

These gatehouses were evidently a key feature of the design, but they had long been something of a mystery, having been largely destroyed in the 1820s. In 1993, the removal of wall-tiles from the then gentlemen's WC revealed medieval masonry which showed that the ground floor of the Kitchen Gate – both the gate-passage and the flanking guardrooms – was largely intact, entirely concealed behind nineteenth-century brickwork and plaster. In addition, fourteenth-century features such as the portcullis groove, doorways and the hanging-position for the great gates, all emerged. It appears, therefore, that the Kitchen Gate was conceived as a fully-defensible gatehouse, even though it was inside the Upper Ward, hard by the big windows of the hall, and led only to the Kitchen courtyard. It seems clear that military architecture was being used here in a self-consciously aesthetic, even romanticised way.

Arches at the back of the Prince of Wales Tower

As early as the fourteenth century, there was an element of fantasy in Edward III's apparently severe architecture.

The other ranges relied for their effect on the contrast between long rows of tall, identical windows, with the vertical accents provided by the towers – probably raised to enhance their effect. The rear wall of the Prince of Wales Tower turned out to consist of fourteenth-century masonry almost for its full height of 23 metres (75 feet); a tall pair of arched recesses found at principal floor level conveyed vividly the scale of the building, and the great size of the windows.

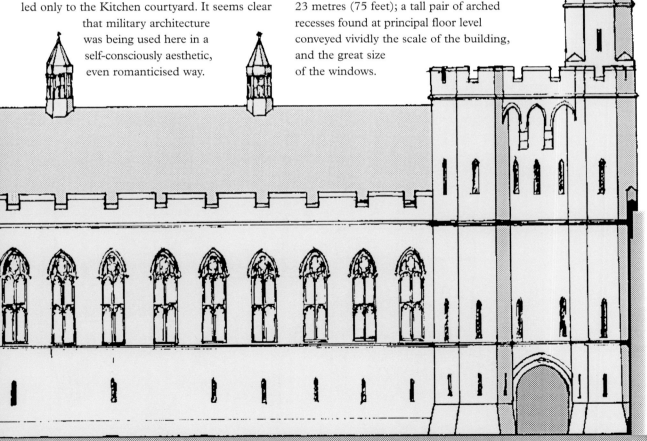

Blocked fourteenth-century doorway, found behind panelling in the Grand Reception Room

ABOVE The Kitchen Court well, with its brick dome

On the north side of the Upper Ward, the palace itself was laid out around three courtyards. The central one represented the old Cloister Court or Spicerie Garden. That to the left (or west), later known as Brick Court, was surrounded by the king and queen's private lodgings. To the east the kitchen and service areas were grouped around the irregularly shaped Kitchen Court. Although the courtyards have long been filled in, this basic tripartite division has governed the development of the State Apartments ever since. Since 1992, a lot more evidence has been gleaned about the fourteenth-century palace, but formidable difficulties remain in interpreting it. The most common medieval house-plan, whether for a large farmhouse or a great mansion, consisted of a hall occupying the middle of the house, with the solar or lord's chamber at the upper or 'dais' end, and the entrance and the kitchen at the lower or 'screens' end. There are many variations on this theme, but the majority of surviving medieval domestic buildings can be understood in these basic terms.

Windsor cannot be understood in these terms at all; hall, kitchen and entrance were all widely separated. Furthermore, all the principal apartments were at first-floor level, one opening out of another, more like the state-rooms of a great seventeenth- or eighteenth-century house, than a 'standard' medieval building. It is not even clear how one reached the Hall from the main entrance; it must have been quite a long route, including a flight of steps at some (unknown) point. A large and impressive blocked doorway was found in the corner of the present Grand Reception Room, and this seems likely to represent part of that main route in. The 'food route' from the Kitchen to the Hall, across a courtyard and up a level, is also uncertain; there seem to be two possible routes, and the answer may be that both were used, depending on the circumstances.

In the classic medieval house plan, the lord's private chambers were behind the upper or 'dais' end of the Hall. This cannot have been the case at Windsor (anyway, it is not clear which end was the dais end). Most of the king and queen's lodgings were outside the fire restoration area, and so we do not have further evidence for them, with the important exception of the king's private chamber in the Rose Tower, discussed on pages 44–45. The plan provided here is our present interpretation of the likely arrangement of the fourteenth-century palace; it represents a

RIGHT A conjectural reconstruction of the medieval Kitchen Court, with the Great Kitchen on the left, and the chapel and Larderie Passage on the right

substantial rewriting of Sir William Hope's version of 1913, but much more interpretative work is required before a full picture can emerge.

Down in the Kitchen Court, the excavation revealed complex evidence of a succession of buildings inside the courtyard. The first set of foundations seemed to relate to a covered passageway leading across the courtyard from the kitchen, perhaps of Henry III's reign. The stone plinth of a large building was found, possibly of the fourteenth century. A rather slighter foundation seemed to indicate a sixteenth-century building, probably timber-framed, and probably that shown in Hollar's aerial view. In the late seventeenth or early eighteenth century, the red brick New or Privy Kitchen was built. This was successively re-faced, re-fenestrated, gutted and rebuilt, then burnt out in 1992.

The royal kitchen had several departments, which must always have been cramped in this small area; we know their names from the accounts: the dressour, the salting-house, the larderye (for meat), the bakehouse, the pasterye (for desserts). With further study, we may be able to attach names to rooms or areas.

The fourteenth-century accounts also referred to the 'great well next the great kitchen', and it was expected that the excavation would reveal this. In due course, the top of the well was indeed found, almost 3 metres in diameter and lined in fine greensand ashlar masonry. It had been covered over with a brick dome, with stairs down and a door for access, probably in the late seventeenth century. In the 1820s, it was filled up with builders' rubble and forgotten. Rediscovered, and now accessible, this was one of the most satisfying finds of the post-fire restoration.

Plans of the ground and principal floors in the fourteenth century

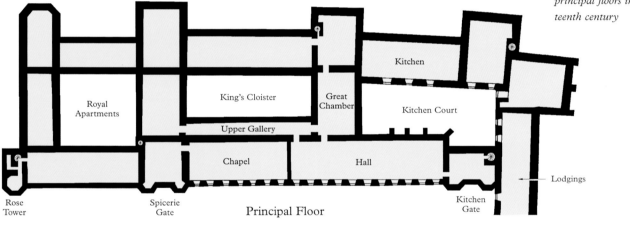

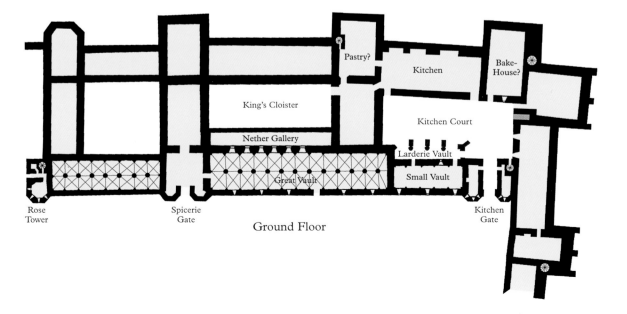

ABOVE A fourteenth-century timber doorway in the Round Tower

RIGHT Fourteenth-century glazed floor tiles, from the Governor's House

Edward III's rebuilding created a great series of apartments at principal floor level, but successive alterations had removed all visible signs of the fourteenth-century interiors. Now, however, there is enough new evidence to start piecing together a picture of what they looked like.

Other than the Hall and Chapel, which were distinguished by their high-pitched roofs, and the Great Chamber, Edward III's interiors were all about the same height (approx. 7m), and mostly of similar widths (approx 7.2m). All seem to have been covered with low-pitched oak-framed roofs; the roof-scar found in the Crimson Drawing Room, indicating a pitch of about 17 degrees, seems to be typical. In most areas, the fourteenth-century roof-timbers have been replaced (they survive above the Garter Throne Room, outside the fire-damaged area). However, we discovered that the seventeenth-century floor-frame of the Grand Reception Room was entirely made up of re-used fourteenth-century roof-timbers. From these we have been able to reconstruct the appearance of the roofs they came from. There seems to have been a uniform style of roof-frame, with close-spaced rafters, chamfered for decorative effect, between low-pitched king-post trusses, and sometimes painted a gold-ochre colour (see page 61).

The principal floor windows were fairly uniform in height. Several of the arched openings were found, but none of the tracery has survived intact. However, we can reconstruct their appearance reasonably accurately from Hollar's views of the Hall and Chapel, and examples in related buildings such as Winchester College and New College, Oxford. Fragments of fourteenth-century painted glass have been found in the Round Tower.

The internal walls were faced in fine ashlar masonry, in white chalk or clunch. It was probably limewashed, not plastered, but most of the important rooms would have been hung with tapestry or fine cloth hangings. However, architectural elements such as door arches and fireplace lintels were generally in a darker greensand stone (such as Reigate stone from

Surrey). This would partly be for structural reasons, but there is some reason to believe that the darker stone was being consciously used for its architectural effect.

Three medieval fireplaces have been found, hidden behind nineteenth-century layers. All are mutilated, but all are very similar, raising the likelihood that they represent a 'Windsor style' of fireplace – flush with the wall, with a massive greensand stone lintel, and a large relieving arch above, also in greensand.

No medieval floor-surfaces were found in the fire-restoration area, but medieval floor tiles

survive in two other places. In a tower-room of the Governor's House, there is an intact fourteenth-century floor of encaustic tiles. In 1992, fourteenth-century tiles were also found beneath a nineteenth-century floor in the second-floor lobby of the octagonal Rose Tower, also known as King John's Tower, at the south-west corner of the State Apartments.

This little room was the scene of the most remarkable discovery of all. In 1992, the removal of the eighteenth-century wood panelling there revealed that the whole room, and the lobby outside, were covered in fourteenth-century painted decoration. The tower seems to have been the private royal entrance to the king's apartments, and also Edward III's private inner sanctum. From documentary sources we knew that the tower was painted in 1365–66, but it was not thought that any of this work had survived.

The scheme consists of an elaborate repetitive pattern meant to cover all of the wall surfaces. This would have been complemented by a decorated tile floor, a fragment of which survived in the corridor outside the painted room. The pattern, painted freehand, is made up of brilliant emerald green cartouches, each of which holds a delicately-painted rose set within flowery borders, all against a deep crimson star-covered background. The pigments appear to match closely those paid for in the accounts for 1365–66, purchased from John Glendale for the painting of La Rose.

List of pigments bought for the decoration of Edward III's private chamber	
12lbs of vertigris, at 12d. per lb	*12s.*
18lbs of red lead, at 18d. per lb	*37s.*
67lbs of white lead, at 6d. per lb	*33s. 6d.*
8lbs of vermilion, at 2s. per lb.	*16s.*
50lbs of broun at 3d. per lb	*12.6d.*
6lbs of vernyssh at 6d. per lb	*4s.*
3lbs of vernyssh at 3d. per lb	*1s. 6d.*
1400 of gold leaf at 6s. per hundred	*£4 4s.*
22 gallons of oil at 2s. a gallon	*44s.*
7lbs. of azure de Bys at 3s. per lb	*21s.*
1qr. 1lb of synciple in bulk	*10s.*

The accounts reveal that the pigments were bought for the painter William Burdon, who received £6 3s. 6d. for 123.5 days' work at 12d. a day. He had five assistants who worked for 77 days at 6d., five others for 75.5 days at 5d., and two who worked at 41 days at 4d. This large, organised workshop system enabled the room to be painted to a high standard quickly and efficiently. The accounts also convey the cost of the scheme, using such expensive materials as gold leaf, blue *bice* (an artificial copper carbonate), vermilion, red lead and *verdigris* (an artificial copper acetate). The pigments listed here were all found in the investigation, except for the gold leaf and the blue *bice*. Also of interest is the

Removal of panelling in King John's Tower revealing the fourteenth-century wall surfaces

use of two different types of varnish, the cheaper one perhaps used to extend the other, which would have originally protected the paintings and given them a rich, saturated appearance.

The design contains roses, as a reference to the dynasty's emblem and to the name of the Rose Tower. It conforms stylistically to a fourteenth-century dating, but is without close parallel in English wall painting. This is only the second royal mural painting to survive from the reign of Edward III, and unlike the fragments from St Stephen's Chapel, Westminster, these ones survive in situ. After the discovery, the panelling was removed, the surviving areas of painting verified, tests carried out, and part of it recorded.

BELOW (left) the original design and colours; (right) at a later stage the walls had been limewashed and the alkalis in the lime have reacted with the acids in the paint to create the 'negative' effect seen here

Maintenance and adaptions

A blocked fifteenth-century window found behind nineteenth-century walling in the Undercroft

After Edward III's mighty rebuilding, the Upper Ward at Windsor remained largely as he left it for three centuries, a testimony to the definitive quality of his work. The most important work in this period was the rebuilding of St George's Chapel in the Lower Ward, begun by Edward IV and completed by Henry VIII. However, the Upper Ward buildings seem to have been large and adaptable enough for succeeding generations to occupy comfortably. Nevertheless, no building of this size and importance can remain entirely static, and new evidence has appeared of the ways in which the palace was maintained and adapted. In the Grand Reception Room, evidence suggests that the room there was remodelled, with a row of new, close-spaced windows high up the west wall; this seems to relate to work done in 1477–78, remaking the roof of the king's great chamber. A fine carved fireplace now in the Steward's Hall bears Edward IV's badge – the rose of York surrounded by the sun's rays – but its original position is not known.

Henry VII is known to have added a tower, with private apartments for himself, at the far (west) end of the palace complex (now occupied by the Royal Library). We now know, from dendrochronological dating, that he also had the kitchen roof rebuilt in 1489 by the master-carpenter John Squyer. There is also evidence for repairs to the kitchen in the Round Tower.

Henry VIII, known for his love of sports and outdoor activities, evidently found the castle's amenities limited, for he built a tennis court at the foot of the Round Tower motte, and he also built the North Wharf or terrace running just beneath the north curtain wall and commanding a tremendous view over the Thames valley. This was originally of timber framing and decking.

Two important works took place during the reigns of Edward VI and Mary. One was the laying of a new water conduit, leading to a great new fountain in the Upper Ward; however, this elaborate system seems to have required heavy maintenance, and no trace of it ever seems to have been found. In 1556–57, Queen Mary extended the lodgings in the Lower Ward for the Poor Knights (now the Military Knights) of Windsor. The buildings still stand, altered but recognisable. Stone was brought from Reading Abbey, and inside the houses there are massive timber frames; in 1993, the opportunity arose to carry out a detailed survey of one of these.

Elizabeth I seems to have been fond of Windsor, and stayed here often. Unlike her father, she was a frugal monarch, and is not remembered as a great builder; her most important building works were at Windsor. In 1570 and 1571 her Clerk of Works, Humphrey Michell, surveyed the castle and made long lists

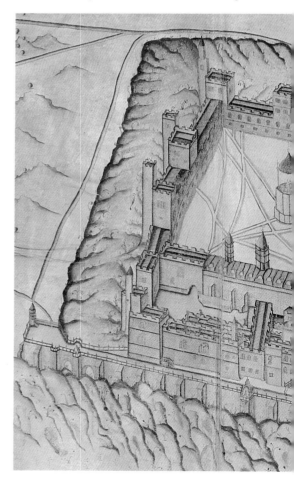

of urgently needed repair works. These were put in hand, and included a major repair to the kitchen roof. Close study and dendrochronological dating have shown that most of the lantern was renewed in 1577. Elizabeth I also had the royal chapel refitted, with new stalls, gallery and a panelled ceiling, as they are shown in a drawing of *c.*1660 by Wenceslas Hollar; no trace of this, however, was found.

Elizabeth I's major works have survived better; in 1575–76 she had her father's timber Wharf rebuilt in stone, as it appears in John Norden's aerial view of the castle of 1609, and as it very largely survives today, with an extension built out by Hugh May in the 1670s. To the west, Elizabeth added the small gallery range, which now houses part of the Royal Library.

In 1629 Charles I had the castle thoroughly surveyed, and once again long lists of urgently required works of maintenance were drawn up by four surveyors, including Inigo Jones. Little,

A drawing of the Royal Chapel, c.1660, *by Wenceslas Hollar showing the panelled ceiling installed for Queen Elizabeth I*

however, seems to have been done. The fine Mannerist sculptor, Nicholas Stone, is known to have worked on a gallery in the chapel, and on a fine gateway from the North Terrace into the park. Nothing of these, though, seems to survive. In 1642 the castle was taken by a Parliamentary garrison and served as a useful prison for captured Royalists. In 1652 the castle narrowly escaped moves in the House of Commons to sell it.

Bird's-eye view of Windsor Castle by John Norden, 1609, showing the North Terrace

CHARLES II & WINDSOR
'The most Romantique castle'

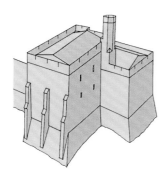

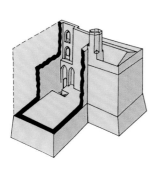

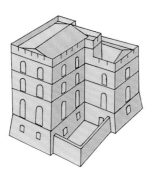

After May's rebuilding

Historical reconstruction sequence: the Board of Green Cloth (now Prince of Wales) Tower

John Kip and Leonard Knyff: Windsor Castle from the south, from Britannia Illustrata, *1711*

The Civil War and Commonwealth were a catastrophe for England's royal palaces; of the twenty or more which had been regularly used under Charles I, more than half were sold, several being demolished outright. Charles II, returning in 1660 to this wasted estate, and with much-reduced financial resources, was obliged to part with several more houses. Windsor had been garrisoned under the Commonwealth, but it was not in good order, and it could so easily have shared the fate of Richmond, Theobalds, Nonsuch and Eltham (to name but four). That it did not is probably because the restored monarchy appreciated the political and symbolic value of what Pepys described in 1666 as 'the most Romantique castle that is in the world'.

As governor of the castle, Charles appointed a great veteran of the Civil War, his cousin Prince Rupert of the Rhine. Prince Rupert moved into the Round Tower, conservatively adapting and redecorating it as his official residence. He carried out some important repairs, notably to the 'carronade' or terrace which surrounds it, and a certain amount of his joinery remains inside. A beautiful watercolour by James Stephanoff, shows the Round Tower's Hall as fitted out by the Prince, with panelling and magnificent displays of weapons. Unfortunately, the room was subdivided by a floor in the nineteenth century.

Charles II, an astute politician with a clear idea of the importance of image, seems to have understood Windsor's value as a symbol of political continuity, legitimacy and sheer longevity. Not only was his father buried there (Wren produced designs for a splendid circular mausoleum at Windsor, never to be built), it was the home of the Garter and of royal ceremonial; Charles re-established the whole panoply of the Garter service and feast at Windsor. Elias Ashmole's *Institutions, Laws and Ceremonies of the Most Noble Order of the Garter*, published in 1672 and including the first real history of the castle, reflected this early antiquarian interest.

The castle, however 'romantique', was hopelessly out of date as a royal residence; work began in 1674. As his architect, Charles chose Hugh May, a gentleman-amateur who had shared the royal exile on the continent. The keynote of May's work at Windsor was a startling deference to the castle's essential medieval character. Startling, because in this period medieval defences were more likely to be regarded as ugly and inconvenient rather than

romantic and historic; one might have expected a king of Charles' generation to demolish the medieval Upper Ward and build a baroque palace from scratch (which is more or less what he did at Winchester in the 1680s). May, however, retained the romantic towered silhouette, piercing the walls with great arched windows. This was not simply for reasons of economy, for examination of the Prince of Wales Tower revealed that May had taken down the outer walls completely, in order to rebuild them with big new windows – to almost exactly the historic height and profile, battlements and all. May also reduced the height of the two fourteenth-century gatehouses flanking the hall and chapel, but reinstated their corbelled parapets to the original design.

On the north side of the kitchen no actual windows were required. Instead, to create a facade, May devised a series of false windows – stone surrounds, with fake windows painted on plaster. This area was enclosed in Wyatville's China Corridor extension during his work, and May's false windows disappeared (May's real windows were all destroyed at the same time). After the fire, one of the painted windows was rediscovered, behind a nineteenth-century cupboard. Although badly damaged, this remarkable find reveals exactly how the Baroque castle was glazed, with white painted timber cross-bars and diamond pane glazing, the upper lights fixed, the lower ones with opening casements. The painted window even shows the kind of festoon curtains used here at the time.

Hugh May, a portrait miniature by Samuel Cooper

The Hall in the Round Tower, watercolour by James Stephanoff, 1819

The Baroque palace

Portrait of Charles II, once the centrepiece of Verrio's dramatic painted ceiling for St George's Hall, cut down in 1826 and rediscovered in 1996

Fabric survey drawing of the window-wall of St George's Hall, showing the discontinuity between the fourteenth-century vaulting bays and the seventeenth-century window bays. The gothic tracery is Wyatville's of the 1820s

Charles II needed elaborate suites of apartments for himself and his Queen, to provide the setting needed for a Baroque court in the age of Versailles. For all the subtle gradations of court etiquette to be observed, both king and queen needed a grand staircase to give access to a guard chamber, an audience chamber, a presence chamber, a drawing room, a state bedchamber, a dressing room, and an inner closet. May could not fit the requisite number of rooms within the shell of the twelfth- and fourteenth-century walls, and his response was to burst out of them – demolishing a long section of the north curtain wall and building a square, barrack-like extension out over the

North Terrace, known as the Star Building from its only decoration, a giant Garter star in gilt lead (long vanished). This was not affected by the 1992 fire. Where the old Great Chamber was, May created the new King's Guard Chamber, and here again, he did not shrink from drastic structural interventions, described above on page 28.

The second phase of Charles II and May's remodelling of the Upper Ward, starting in 1680, was the rebuilding of the medieval hall and chapel. Here again, the removal of panelling and plasterwork after the fire has enabled us to understand what happened. For May, the scale of the medieval building was all wrong; the windows were too small and too narrowly spaced for the grand new rooms he had in mind. He demolished the whole front wall to first floor window-sill level and rebuilt it. May upped the scale, replacing the eighteen medieval window bays, with thirteen larger new ones. This gave him a problem; the medieval Undercroft remained below, its vaults and its windows preserving the fourteenth-century, eighteen-bay pattern. May had to block and re-cut the windows to follow his new thirteen-bay pattern, without disturbing the springing for the vaulting. As a result, the new window openings dive crazily through the wall at oblique angles, sometimes disappearing right behind the vault-ribs.

The Undercroft itself was subdivided with brick partitions in this period, and used for a variety of domestic purposes. At the east end a

series of brick vaults were constructed forming a kind of basement within the Undercroft; these are still in use as the royal wine-cellars. Moving west, one large area of the Undercroft had been left without the brick partitions, and here we found a seventeenth-century Purbeck stone floor beneath later floors. Floor drains, and evidence for wooden partitions were also found, probably relating to some kind of storage use, perhaps for barrels.

At the west end of the Undercroft, we found a lower-floor level with brick paving, again probably of seventeenth-century date. This had drainage channels leading into large glazed pots, set into the floor. These were not drains as such, but seem to have been intended to collect some kind of run-off; it is not yet clear what this mysterious feature is. It was also down in the

Undercroft that we found the threshold of a seventeenth-century brick door with a gold coin, an 'angel' of the reign of Edward IV, set into the mortar. The coin, which was already two centuries old at the time, seems to have been buried there as a charm, to ward off evil spirits.

The medieval kitchen was repaired by May, and its windows re-formed. Despite this, a new brick kitchen was built in the Kitchen Court outside. Its date is not yet clear, but it may well be from the second stage of May's alterations, in the 1680s. The new building spanned the great Kitchen Well, which is probably why the well had to be covered over with a brick dome (see page 43). The New Kitchen was much altered and re-faced in following centuries, and was badly damaged in the 1992 fire, but its walls have been retained in the restoration work.

Painting by Charles Wild of the Baroque St George's Hall, from Pyne's Royal Residences, *1819*

Antonio Verrio

Antonio Verrio (*c*.1639–1707), born in Lecce in southern Italy, arrived in England in 1672, and by 1675 he was working at Windsor. Facts concerning Verrio's early life and training are in short supply, but his work belongs clearly in the Neapolitan baroque tradition of Lanfranco or Luca Giordano. Between 1675 and 1685 he covered about twenty of May's new ceilings with allegorical scenes of gods, goddesses and heroes, celebrating the rule of the House of Stuart. The Hall and Chapel were to be his greatest commission, with both walls and ceilings painted. The new St George's Hall was still dedicated to the Order of the Garter and the Plantagenets, but was re-interpreted for the Baroque age. The whole 33.5-metre (110-foot) length of the north wall was taken up with a victory procession for the Black Prince, greeted by his father Edward III, all figures life-size and dressed in Roman armour, framed between painted Corinthian columns. Verrio may well have been directly inspired for this great composition by Mantegna's celebrated 'Triumphs of Caesar' panels, already in the

Wild's view of the Baroque Chapel, painted just before its destruction by Wyatville to create his St George's Hall

Royal Collection. At the centre of the vast ceiling composition was Charles II himself, carried to heaven by Fame and attendant virtues.

On the north wall of the Chapel, another great composition represented the courtyard of the Temple in Jerusalem, with Christ healing the sick surrounded by a multitude of onlookers. Verrio's 'modello' for this, a highly finished oil painting, survives in the Royal Collection. Hall and Chapel were further adorned with splendid carved woodwork by Grinling Gibbons. Together, these rooms were the most splendid painted interiors ever created in Britain, barring only the Painted Hall at Greenwich (painted a generation later by Sir James Thornhill).

The fire burnt away much of Wyatville's lath and plaster in the eastern half of the Hall, revealing bare masonry underneath. Verrio's painting, apparently, had also been on plaster supported on timber studwork, not directly on the wall. Wyatville, it seemed, had destroyed it completely, except for surviving fragments found in the window embrasures. Wyatville's plasterwork survived in the western part of the Hall, and at a comparatively late stage in the restoration work, holes were being cut to make ready for the new oak ceiling. To general astonishment, it became clear that areas of Verrio's mural of 'Christ Healing the Sick' had indeed survived, covered up for 170 years by Wyatville's lath and plaster. Further opening-up was done; sadly, only fragments of Verrio's great work survived at high level – his painted cornice, areas of his painted architecture, a figure clinging to a column and faces looking over a parapet, but none of the main figures in the scene.

These areas were cleaned and conserved by English Heritage's Painting Conservation Studio, and recorded; it became clear that they

matched the 'modello' exactly. However, there was too little left, and it was too high up, to justify taking steps to leave it on display. The surviving fragments are now re-sealed behind modern plasterwork, but a detailed photographic record has been made.

By a wonderful coincidence, shortly after this discovery another fragment of Verrio's great lost masterpiece was found, this time in a Vienna auction-room catalogue. The London art-dealer Philip Mould recognised a portrait of Charles II, wrongly catalogued as a portrait of the Emperor Leopold I and wrongly attributed, and bought it. The portrait turned out to be painted on a panel of lath and plaster, and writing on the back identified it as from Windsor. Research has established beyond doubt that this is, indeed, the focal point of Verrio's vast ceiling-composition in the Hall, which someone had the foresight to cut out and save. This amazing find has been bought by the Royal Collection, and returned to Windsor (see page 50).

A fragment of Verrio's decoration, showing a figure clinging to a column

Conservation work in progress on the Verrio fragments

'Christ Healing the Sick': Verrio's 'modello' for the north wall of the Chapel

THE ROYAL COLLECTION © HER MAJESTY THE QUEEN

GEORGE IV & WYATVILLE

Windsor restored

After the Hanoverian succession of 1714, Windsor slumbered in slightly run-down obscurity for over 60 years. For reasons which are not clear, George I and George II never resided there, most of the castle being occupied as grace-and-favour apartments. From about 1775 onwards George III rediscovered the castle and its magnificent parks, and in 1786 he moved back into the state apartments. In 1800 a limited renovation of the Upper Ward buildings was begun, generally restoring gothic detailing to the exterior, to designs by James Wyatt, but the work was halted by the king's final descent into madness in 1811. Thereafter, until his death in 1820, he was kept here in seclusion. The Prince Regent then ascended the throne as George IV. He was one of the most cultured (and extravagant) men ever to sit on a throne, and almost immediately he sought the government's support for two great projects – the renovation of Windsor and the remodelling of Buckingham House as Buckingham Palace.

A limited competition led to the selection of Jeffry Wyatt, a notable country-house architect

TOP RIGHT George IV dressed in medieval armour, in a portrait sketch by Sir Thomas Lawrence, 1814

RIGHT Sir Jeffry Wyatville, by Sir Thomas Lawrence

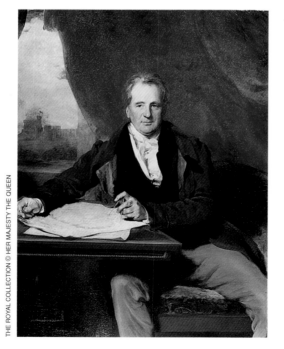

and member of a celebrated architectural dynasty; he shortly changed his surname to Wyatville to distinguish himself from his many relations. Wyatville was a pliable, affable figure, a brilliant improviser more than a creative genius. His work at Windsor closely followed a brief drawn up in 1824 by the king, and more particularly by his adviser Sir Charles Long. The creation of new royal apartments in the east and south ranges, the creation of the Grand Corridor to improve the circulation, the addition of an extra storey for servants' accommodation, the new George IV Gateway, and the raising of the Round Tower to 'improve' the castle's skyline, were all in Long's original memorandum. To a large degree, Wyatville's role was to interpret and execute the king and Long's vision – which was more a romantic and literary, than a historical one.

Outside, Wyatville heightened and dramatised the skyline for deliberate picturesque effect, far beyond what it had been; the roof-parapet of the Grand Reception Room was raised by over 2 metres purely for scenic reasons and the result labelled the Cornwall Tower. At the north-east corner he demolished a twelfth-century tower which had structural problems and built the very high, octagonal Brunswick Tower instead. Several of the towers were provided with dramatically corbelled and machicolated parapets, which Edward III would never have recognised. The most dramatic intervention of this kind was the doubling in height of the Round Tower in 1830–31. The original twelfth-century shell was 'sleeved' – thickened with a brick lining – so it could support the tremendous additional weight. The result was like no medieval tower ever built – the newly raised walls were completely hollow. The resulting skyline has become justly celebrated – it is one of the greatest works of art of the Picturesque movement in Britain.

Even though the budget for Wyatville's work spiralled upwards, the project remained a popular one, far more so than the remodelling of Buckingham Palace. Windsor was a national

icon, and 'restoring' its character as a castle was a popular cause. This was the age of *Ivanhoe* (published in 1819, and a great favourite of George IV's), and a renewed fascination with the Middle Ages. Windsor's close association with Edward III and his victories in France would have made it all the more appealing to a generation flushed with the successes of Trafalgar and Waterloo.

LEFT The hollow interior of the Round Tower, before 1989

BELOW Wyatville's 'before and after' views of the north side of the Upper Ward, 1824. The fire damaged the left-hand quarter of this view

Wyatville's timber and iron roof structures after the fire

The Kitchen Cloister, added by Edward Blore, 1841–42

Damaged decorative plasterwork in Blore's Private Chapel

One of the cast-iron trusses stamped with Bramah's mark

When Wyatville began work in 1824, his budget was set at £150,000; this was soon exhausted, and in 1826 the commissioners for the rebuilding added another £100,000. Wyatville explained that wherever he had opened up floors, panelling and roofs, he had found rotten timbers and structural defects, which required urgent attention, leading him to do more opening up, and so on. Investigation revealed just how far he had gone.

The Industrial Revolution was gathering pace, and Wyatville had the benefit of new iron-founding and building technologies. Over much of the ground floor he stripped out the timber floors, replacing them with brick jack-arches over cast-iron beams to make fireproof floors, similar to contemporary warehouse construction but with timber joists and floorboards sitting on top. Many of Wyatville's iron beams were damaged in the 1992 fire and had to be taken out. Some of them were simply of cast iron, but many were of a more sophisticated design: a cast-iron body, with a channel in the underside into which was set a long wrought-iron rod, under tension, to give the whole beam greater tensile strength.

In the Prince of Wales Tower, Sir Charles Long's brief called for a great new State Dining Room, in place of four smaller rooms. To light it, Wyatville had to break a large hole through the front wall, a potentially risky business. To span this, the firm of Bramah & Son made an extraordinary cast-iron truss, again tensioned with wrought-iron rods. Thankfully, this survived the fire in good condition, and remains in situ. Iron was expensive, and most of Wyatville's roof structures were of timber, queen-post trusses with iron straps and bolts for reinforcement. Several were irretrievably badly damaged in 1992, but they were recorded while being dismantled.

George IV and Long's demands for large new state-rooms on the east front posed numerous structural problems. For instance, Wyatville had effectively hollowed out the Prince of Wales Tower to create the State Dining Room, and this left him an engineering dilemma – how to construct two floors-worth of servants' bedrooms above it, without any support from below. His response was to build huge timber trusses spanning the tower at second floor and roof level, and to hang the second floor and the State Dining Room ceiling from these with the help of wrought-iron rods. This ingenious solution was itself destroyed by a fire in 1853, after which Anthony Salvin restored the Tower. Salvin wanted his construction to be fire-proof, and inserted massive wrought-iron beams to span its width. These beams were particularly interesting, representing the last generation of the large-scale use of hand-wrought iron, before it was rendered obsolete by the advent of mass-produced steel after 1856. Sadly, the beams were badly damaged in the 1992 fire, and all had to come out. Thus, in addition to its medieval history, the Prince of Wales Tower also embodied two generations of innovative nineteenth-century engineering.

Wyatville managed to find sources of Bagshot Heath stone for the external walls, but behind this, his walls entirely consist of hard-baked stock brick. For architectural detailing, he used great quantities of yellow-brown Bath stone, brought by canal from the west of England.

Wyatville went on working at Windsor after George IV's death, even though the new king William IV had relatively little interest in the place. Work was still going on when Wyatville died in 1840, by which time over £800,000 had been spent there.

Yet the castle was still not suited to royal needs. Edward Blore succeeded Wyatville as architect, and made numerous alterations for Queen Victoria. The Kitchen Court was filled in with an elegant little top-lit cloister of Bath stone. The Kitchen Gatehouse was blocked up, falling into use as storerooms and ultimately lavatories, from which oblivion it has only recently been rescued. In the area above, Blore and the sculptor John Thomas converted Wyatville's Band Room (a somewhat unsatisfactory ante-room where the orchestra played during banquets) into a new Private Chapel. Heavy plaster decoration of gothic tracery was put up, nearly all of it destroyed, or damaged beyond repair, in the fire.

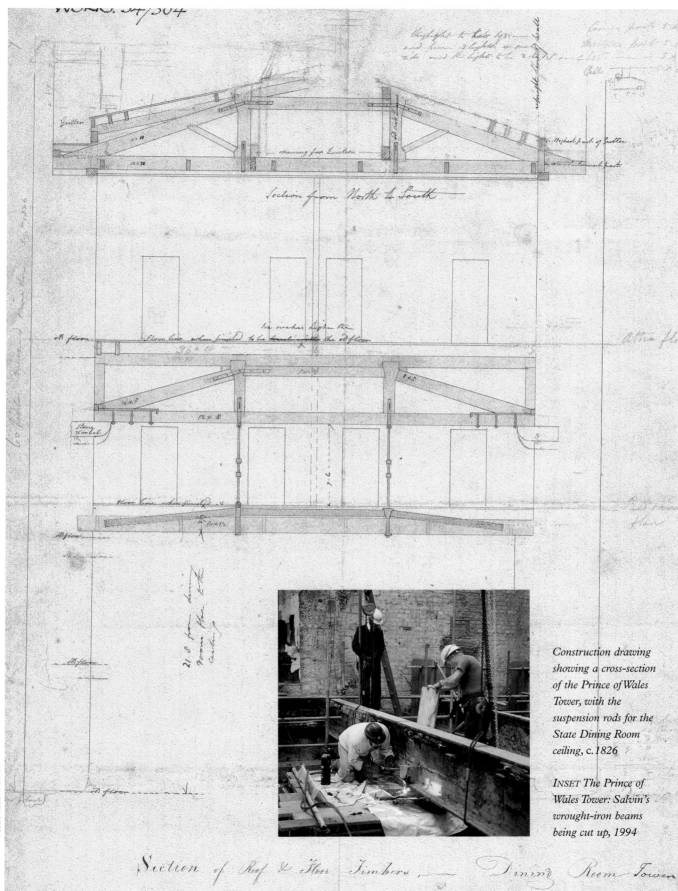

Guttor

Section from North to South

Section of Roof & Floor Timbers, — Dining Room Tower

Construction drawing showing a cross-section of the Prince of Wales Tower, with the suspension rods for the State Dining Room ceiling, c.1826

INSET The Prince of Wales Tower: Salvin's wrought-iron beams being cut up, 1994

Regency taste

Gothic wallpaper of c.1825–30, found behind a fitted cupboard

A charred figure of St George and the Dragon from the Hall

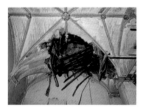

Damaged ceiling over the Equerries' Staircase show-ing the original lath and plaster construction, painted to resemble Bath stone

RIGHT St George's Hall before the fire

George IV was a notoriously demanding and capricious patron; left to himself, Wyatville would certainly have preferred to have made all the new interiors gothic. As it was, in many areas the king's francophile tastes dictated otherwise. Wyatville's greatest triumph was over St George's Hall, where he persuaded the commissioners to agree to the destruction of May and Verrio's Baroque hall and chapel, replacing them with the present immensely long room, decorated in his somewhat mechanical style.

The budget for the new interior was very limited, and the 1992 fire laid bare Wyatville's economies and short-cuts with brutal clarity. The vast ceiling, for instance, painted to resemble a late-medieval oak roof, was made entirely of plasterwork by Francis Bernasconi & Company. The ceiling was jerry-built; in order to make up

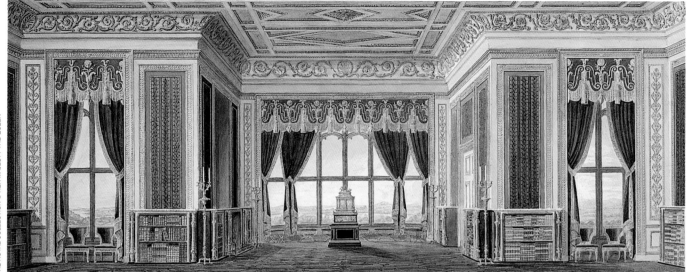

the beams and bosses, huge thicknesses of solid plaster had been cast onto armatures made of thin timber battens, nails and 6-inch spikes, wound about with coarse string. All of this had collapsed during the fire. Wyatville lined the walls with lath and plaster, but this was then painted to resemble fine ashlar masonry, with lines drawn on the surface to represent the joints. Sand was thrown into the paint, to give it a texture similar to the Bath stone being used outside. Wyatville designed some of the circulation areas in the gothic style, such as the Equerries' Staircase. He was also responsible for the State Dining Room and the Octagon Room, for which the 15-year-old AWN Pugin was employed to design sideboards and chairs.

Elsewhere, the rich French-inspired style favoured by the king held sway. George IV was a great collector of Dutch and Flemish pictures, and of French furniture and decorative art of the eighteenth century. As Regent, he had rebuilt Carlton House on Pall Mall, creating a magnificent sequence of state-rooms to house his collections.

By the time he ascended the throne, George had become bored with Carlton House, which had structural problems, and which was too small to house full Court entertainments. In 1827, Carlton House was demolished, and many of its fittings taken to Windsor. The suite of three drawing rooms – White, Green and Crimson – which Wyatville created in the east wing, were decorated by the firm of Morel & Seddon, using many of the salvaged items, such as fireplaces, bookcases, and wonderful carved door trophies, as well as much of the furniture. These rooms may indeed be described as the ghost of Carlton House.

The king's taste for French decorative art was also the key to the creation of the Grand Reception Room (pictured on page 29). The king had a circle of friends and art dealers who periodically made purchases on his behalf, and in 1825 Sir Charles Long bought some splendid Louis XV panelling, and a set of superb Gobelins tapestries depicting the story of Jason and the Golden Fleece for him in Paris. The room was always believed to have been designed around these purchases, but prior to the 1992 fire, it had not been clear how much of the story was actually true. In 1994, the layers of paint were cleaned off as part of the restoration work. It immediately became clear that the actual panelling rose about three-quarters of the way up the room, while the top quarter was lath-and-plaster, moulded to match. Extra ornament (made in lime-putty composition) had been added to the genuine panelling, to suit the richer taste of the 1820s. There seems no reason to doubt that the panelling is indeed genuine French *boiserie* of about 1750, much enriched. A magnificent rococo ceiling by Francis Bernasconi & Company, the swan-song of the Italian *stuccadori* in England, completed the ensemble. The room as a whole is a fascinating object lesson in the history of taste, and in the way one age influences another.

Morel & Seddon's design for George IV's Library, now the Green Drawing Room, 1826

A damaged door from the Crimson Drawing Room, showing one of the superb carved 'Carlton House' trophy panels by Edward Wyatt

Plasterwork in the Grand Reception Room added to the eighteenth-century French panelling

THE FUTURE

Analysis & publication

Graffiti representing a woman and a cross, in the Governor's House

Graffiti in the form of a puzzle, as yet undeciphered, in the Larderie Passage

RIGHT Charles Wild's watercolour of the King's Guard Chamber for Pyne's Royal Residences, *1819, a room which was remodelled by Wyatville to create the Grand Reception Room. Historic views such as this provide valuable documentary evidence of the previous appearance of rooms which can be linked to written historical sources and the evidence from survey and excavation*

One of the most dramatic effects of the fire, as we have seen, was to expose the complex history concealed beneath the often rather bland nineteenth-century surfaces. Five years of sifting, excavation and survey work of all kinds has transformed our view of the castle and provided us with a vast body of new information, and a large 'material archive' of finds.

Thousands of fragments were salvaged from the site, but were too damaged to be reincorporated in the building; many of these have specific historic interest but little or no real monetary value, and steps have been taken to find an appropriate home for some of them. These range from a great iron roof-truss from above St George's Hall, which has been donated by the Royal Household to the Science Museum, to samples of the castle's historic window mechanisms which have been donated to the Brooking Collection at the University of

Greenwich. The more conventional archaeological finds, such as medieval tiles, glass fragments, pottery, bone fragments and seeds, remain with English Heritage for the time being, for scientific analysis.

Indeed, much more work remains to be done, analysing the finds and the survey work, and reviewing the documentary sources. By trying to tie all these different facets together we hope that we can gain a deeper understanding of the castle's history in much greater detail than can be outlined here. Details gleaned from excavation and survey can be tied in with documentary sources, whether written, such as the repairs to the Great Kitchen roof in 1489 revealed by dendrochronology, or visual sources such as those showing rooms since remodelled by Wyatville. Scientific analysis will help identify and date finds.

We hope that this process will shed new light on the functions of different areas, on the building methods used at the castle, the diet and way of life of those who lived there, and how all of these changed over the years. In due course a major academic monograph will appear. In the meantime, the findings presented here are provisional; they will certainly be added to, and they may have to be corrected.

It is understandable that, prior to the 1992 fire, Windsor Castle was often seen as primarily a nineteenth-century creation; no less an authority than the *History of the King's Works* could judge that 'Windsor Castle today is to all intents and purposes a nineteenth-century creation, and it stands as the image of what the early nineteenth-century thought a castle should be'. Even if that was all it was, Windsor would still be important and interesting; Wyatville's work is one of the greatest achievements of the Picturesque Gothic, and the state-rooms are masterpieces of late Georgian taste.

As we now know, the truth is a great deal more complex. Out of the disaster of November 1992 has come a vastly enhanced understanding of the castle's history. What is more, strenuous efforts have been made as part of the restoration project to leave much more of the hidden medieval masonry visible, so the building can also speak for itself; in the words of a member of the Royal Household, to make it 'feel' more like a castle.

J R PIDGEON

ABOVE The evidence gleaned from the excavation and survey work will allow us to produce more interpretative reconstructions of the construction and past uses of rooms in the castle, such as this reconstruction drawing by John Pidgeon of the principal floor room in the east lodging range, now the Crimson Drawing Room, in the fourteenth century

LEFT The now reunited Undercroft, after the removal of partition walls, one of the most statisfying historical outcomes of the restoration work

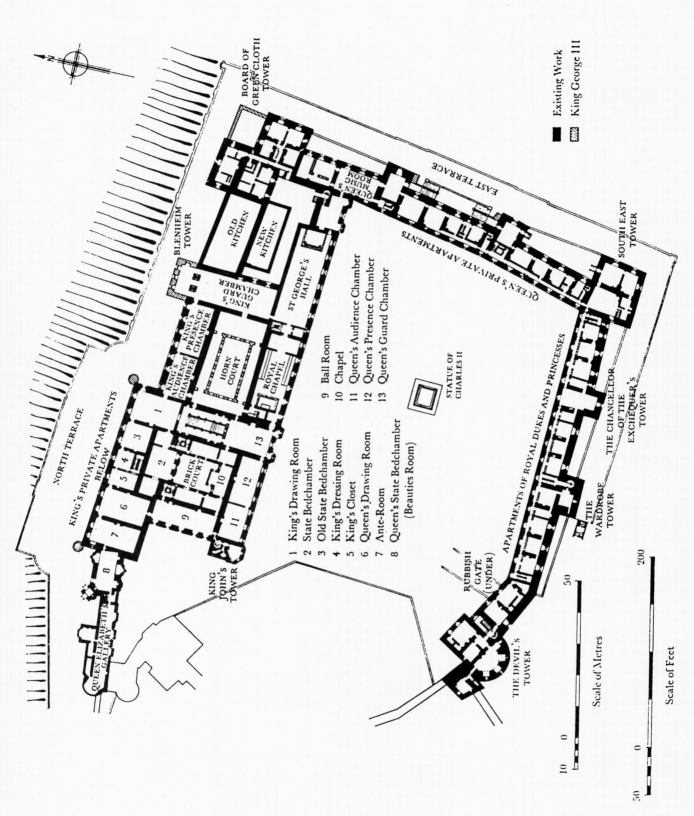

BOARD OF GREEN CLOTH TOWER

BLENHEIM TOWER

OLD KITCHEN

NEW KITCHEN

QUEEN'S MUSIC ROOM

EAST TERRACE

SOUTH EAST TOWER

KING'S GUARD CHAMBER

ST GEORGE'S HALL

KING'S PRESENCE CHAMBER

KING'S AUDIENCE CHAMBER

HORN COURT

ROYAL CHAPEL

BRICK COURT

NORTH TERRACE

KING'S PRIVATE APARTMENTS BELOW

QUEEN'S PRIVATE APARTMENTS

QUEEN ELIZABETH'S GALLERY

KING JOHN'S TOWER

1 King's Drawing Room
2 State Bedchamber
3 Old State Bedchamber
4 King's Dressing Room
5 King's Closet
6 Queen's Drawing Room
7 Ante-Room
8 Queen's State Bedchamber
   (Beauties Room)

9 Ball Room
10 Chapel
11 Queen's Audience Chamber
12 Queen's Presence Chamber
13 Queen's Guard Chamber

STATUE OF CHARLES II

APARTMENTS OF ROYAL DUKES AND PRINCESSES

RUBBISH GATE (UNDER)

THE DEVIL'S TOWER

THE WARDROBE TOWER

THE CHANCELLOR OF THE EXCHEQUER'S TOWER

Scale of Metres

10   0   50

Scale of Feet

50   0   200

Existing Work

King George III

The Upper Ward in about 1800

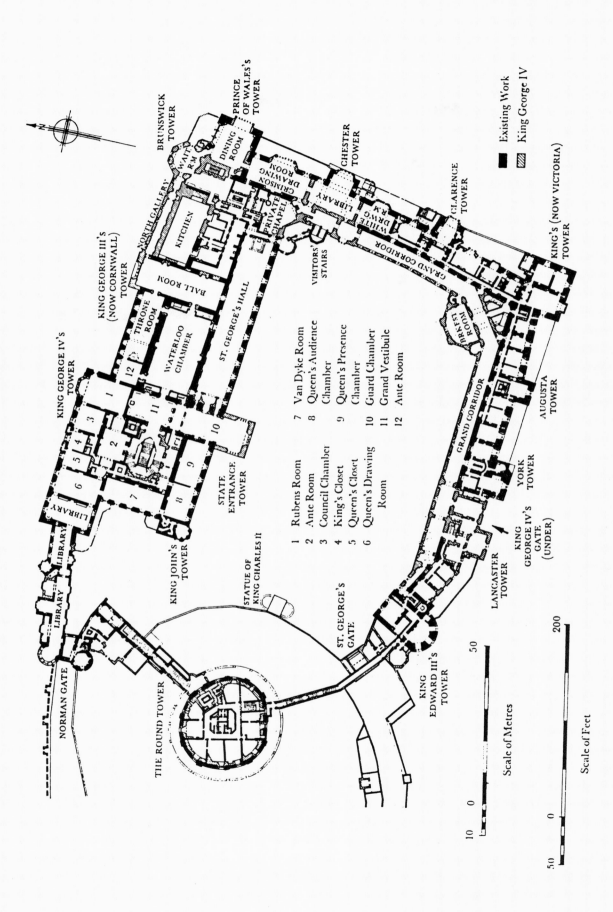

BRUNSWICK TOWER

PRINCE OF WALES'S TOWER

KING GEORGE III'S (NOW CORNWALL) TOWER

NORTH GALLERY

WAIT. RM

DINING ROOM

CHESTER TOWER

CRIMSON DRAWING ROOM

PRIVATE CHAPEL

LIBRARY

KITCHEN

WHITE DRWG R.M

CLARENCE TOWER

BALL ROOM

KING GEORGE IV'S TOWER

THRONE ROOM

VISITORS' STAIRS

WATERLOO CHAMBER

ST. GEORGE'S HALL

GRAND CORRIDOR

KING'S (NOW VICTORIA) TOWER

12

1

11

10

3

5   4

2

BRKFST ROOM

LIBRARY

6

9

KING JOHN'S TOWER

7

8

STATE ENTRANCE TOWER

GRAND CORRIDOR

AUGUSTA TOWER

1   Rubens Room
2   Ante Room
3   Council Chamber
4   King's Closet
5   Queen's Closet
6   Queen's Drawing Room

7   Van Dyke Room
8   Queen's Audience Chamber
9   Queen's Presence Chamber
10 Guard Chamber
11 Grand Vestibule
12 Ante Room

YORK TOWER

KING GEORGE IV'S GATE (UNDER)

STATUE OF KING CHARLES II

LANCASTER TOWER

ST. GEORGE'S GATE

NORMAN GATE

LIBRARY

LIBRARY

THE ROUND TOWER

KING EDWARD III'S TOWER

N

■ Existing Work

▨ King George IV

Scale of Metres

10   0   50

Scale of Feet

50   0   200

The Upper Ward after Wyatville's remodelling, 1843

Further reading

The History of the King's Works, H M Colvin (general editor): Vols I & II, *The Middle Ages* (1963); Vol. III, *1485–1660*, Part 1 (1975); Vol. IV, *1485–1660*, Part 2 (1982); Vol. V, *1660–1782* (1976); Vol. VI, *1782–1851* (1973)

Girouard, Mark, *Windsor – the Most Romantic Castle* (Hodder & Stoughton, 1993)

Hope, Sir William St John, *Windsor Castle* (2 vols, Country Life, 1913)

Linstrum, Derek, *Sir Jeffry Wyatville* (Clarendon Press, 1972)

Morshead, Sir Owen, *Windsor Castle* (Phaidon, 1951)

Nicolson, Adam, *Restoration* (Michael Joseph, 1997)

Robinson, J M, *Windsor Castle* (Royal Collection, 1994)

Rowse, A L, *Windsor Castle in the History of the Nation* (Weidenfeld & Nicolson, 1974)

Watkin, David, *The Royal Interiors of Regency England* (J M Dent & Sons, 1977)

Index